Kate James is uniquely qualified to  life issues like building confidence, fi personal strengths, values and needs.

Having experienced a few career cha.... ....ne understands the dissatisfaction in people unsure of their personal or career paths.

As a sought-after mindfulness expert, with over 30 years of meditation practice, Kate helps her clients focus on what really matters. She facilitates workshops and retreats online, in Melbourne and Byron Bay, and continues her own studies into positive psychology, Acceptance and Commitment Therapy (ACT), mind-fulness and self-compassion. Her teaching draws on the science and psychology of meditation and her aim is to make mindfulness accessible and enjoyable for people from all walks of life.

Her one-on-one clients range from lawyers to artists, entrepre-neurs to corporate leaders. Most are creative in some way or want to learn how to be. All are down-to-earth, sensitive and insightful people who have an interest in living their own version of a purposeful and meaningful life. Many are transitioning (or have transitioned) out of corporate roles into their own creative startups.

Kate has first-hand experience of the life balance challenge, having spent the past 32 years juggling marriage, motherhood and a successful career.

Kate is the author of five bestselling personal development books including *Be Mindful and Simplify Your Life* and *Create Calm*. Her guided meditations have been listened to over three million times on the free Insight Timer meditation app.

# Change Your Thinking *to* Change Your Life

*A practical guide to finding your purpose*

## KATE JAMES

MACMILLAN
Pan Macmillan Australia

*For all of our vulnerable selves.*

*'I wish I could show you when you are lonely or in darkness
the astonishing light of your own being.'*
Hafiz, 14th century Persian poet

# Contents

# Introduction

The room I work in has a view of the garden. When I spend four hours here with a client, often a kookaburra joins us in the tree outside the window or a family of ducks wanders onto the lawn.

It's the perfect setting to reflect on your life. Here, my client shares their story and together we explore their values, uncover limiting beliefs and consider what will make for a purposeful life.

While everyone's story is different, the people I work with share many similar qualities. They are deep thinkers who often describe themselves as sensitive. Many lean towards introversion and almost all want to make a contribution to society in some way. They care about and want to contribute to the wellbeing of others, they value the health of society as a whole and they are thoughtful in the way they interact with the environment. They seek out genuine, authentic connections and feel compelled to be doing something meaningful with their lives. Despite the fact that almost all have achieved a good degree of success, they're usually pretty hard on themselves. They are prone to imposter syndrome (the feelings of inadequacy that persist despite their success), perfectionism or generally just not feeling good enough.

They are humble people who care about making this world a better place, yet for whatever reason, they have found themselves lost, directionless or doubting their ability.

All are people who recognise the importance of finding a balance between appreciating what they have now and wanting to improve themselves. They're curious about how to develop self-acceptance, how to find a greater sense of harmony in the present moment and how to move forward in a purposeful, meaningful way.

They're people who are just like I was in my early life: experiencing self-doubt, unclear about their direction and unsure about where to turn to find clarity. More often than not, they've found themselves on a life path almost by accident. They studied something they were good at, landed their first job and their career and lives have just happened.

This was me until my mid-thirties. I had no idea what I wanted from my life, other than wanting to become a mother. I didn't feel I had the option to make 'homemaker' a career choice and I had a great sense of insecurity about my lack of direction. I fell into different roles without giving any consideration to a long-term career plan. It wasn't until our daughters started school that I really began to think about what I wanted to do for work.

By then I was employed as a business manager for filmmakers and completing a business degree, majoring in marketing. I loved the people I worked with, didn't mind the work I was doing and for the most part enjoyed my course. But I had a strong sense that this wasn't really the true path for me.

I wasn't one of those people who had clarity about a single passion. My interests were so varied. I loved science and the human mind and I was interested in business. I was curious about creativity, spirituality, nature, gardening and cooking. I started film school, took a photography course, worked in a garden centre, and considered graphic design, catering, psychology and counselling.

I was literally all over the place.

I would probably have continued this way had it not been for a few pivotal moments that changed the course of my life.

In the early 1990s, my freelancing film-technician husband, Chris, was out of work for a few months. My part-time job covered our basic expenses but it wasn't enough to pay the bills. I was stressed and anxious about money and the uncertainty ahead of us and I started to become irritable with Chris and our daughters.

I had no control over Chris's work situation or our financial situation but I knew I *could* manage how I responded. I wanted to be calm and grounded for everyone.

In a moment of clarity, I realised I needed to stop looking outside myself for harmony and reconnect with the things that I loved. I put my business degree on hold and planted a herb and vegetable garden. I started baking my own bread and making preserves, and we raised a few chickens in our small backyard. I read about spirituality and all the alternative things I had loved as a teenager. The same things that had made me feel like an outsider in my younger years were now helping me go within.

Instead of trying to conform to what I believed to be society's version of success, I began to connect with the truest part of myself and I discovered I knew one thing. I didn't want a mainstream career or life. I wanted to find my own path.

I enrolled in a meditation course and committed to a twice-daily practice. As well as quieting my mind and helping me to find inner stillness, I began to understand myself in a way that I hadn't before. I worked with a psychologist who helped me discover my own set of values and beliefs and how my patterns of thinking and my behaviours were impacting my relationships and my life choices.

As my self-awareness grew, I realised that helping other people learn about who they are and what matters most to them is what I wanted to do too.

While researching psychology courses, I stumbled across an article in the newspaper about coaching, a new industry in Australia and something I'd not heard of before. In what was the first of a series of serendipitous events, I then discovered that the international coaching school featured in the article had its head office only a few doors from where I lived.

I knew I had found what I would do with my life. I could see how to combine my business experience with my love of creativity and interest in the human mind. I would coach creative business owners and those who wanted to transition into their own business. I would help people find their own passions and discover their inner wisdom. I would help people find their way home to themselves.

I enrolled in the training and launched my own business.

Over the years, I have found a way to combine all the things I love. I studied positive psychology, Acceptance and Commitment Therapy, mindfulness, self-compassion, Internal Family Systems,

Buddhism, spirituality and the healing powers of nature, and I read about 'the connectedness of all things'. I take clients to beautiful places where we meditate together and immerse ourselves in the natural environment, and I've carved out a simple life where I cook and garden and spend time with the people I love.

The clients I work with these days share the same desire I had – to understand themselves well and to learn how to be the most authentic, grounded versions of themselves as they seek to pursue a life that they love.

Throughout the book, I'll share the insights, teachings and practical steps that have helped me the most over the years. I'll share a little of my story and I'll tell you about some of my clients, too. All their names have been changed and most case studies are a composite of several clients' stories to protect people's privacy.

Many of the ideas I introduce draw on other people's wisdom. Like many who work in this space, I consider myself a life-long learner and in many ways, still a beginner on this path of self-discovery.

You might think of this book as your alternative to joining me in the room with a view of the garden. I'll take you through many of the exercises I have offered my clients over the years.

My hope is that there'll be something in these pages that will help you to find your way back to yourself, overcome the beliefs that limit your life choices and guide to your version of a peaceful and positive life.

## How to use this book

Something I've learned from reading hundreds of self-help books over the years is that they're full of great ideas that I imagine putting into practice *later*, but often, later doesn't come around.

My hope is that this book might be different for you.

There are two sections to the book. The first will help you get to know yourself well and the second will help you overcome the thoughts and beliefs that inhibit inner peace and will then help you find your way to your version of a fulfilling life.

Within each chapter, I've included case studies and exercises to help you understand how the concepts can be applied in your own life. I've also included my own examples so you have an idea of how I bring these concepts together to create a composite of my 'authentic self'.

If you notice that you judge or compare yourself to others as you respond to some questions, be aware that your ego is the part of your mind that decides if your attributes are 'good' or 'bad'. Try to approach the questions with a sense of openness and remind yourself that like everyone, you have positive attributes and negative ones. When you learn to fully acknowledge and accept your strengths *and your weaknesses*, you'll discover a more balanced state of mind where you can simply say, 'This is who I am'.

The reality is that we are all inherently flawed – just as we're all inherently good. When we're able to accept ourselves as we are, and give ourselves permission to embrace all of our unique attributes as well as the interests we feel genuinely connected to, we start to become the most authentic and best version of ourselves.

Only then can you create a life that is truly right for you.

I encourage you to complete every exercise as you read each chapter. Ideally, keep a journal with you as you're reading, so you have all your notes in one place. I'll be introducing concepts you have more than likely encountered before, but I'm extending the invitation for you to be very honest with yourself as you consider them this time. If you're not completely clear about a response, scribble down your first thoughts and reflect on your answers for a day or two. Even just the initial step of getting an idea out of your head onto paper will stimulate your thinking and help you to know yourself better.

I recommend handwriting your notes rather than putting them into your phone or your computer. There are studies that tell us that writing by hand helps engage the prefrontal cortex, giving you a better chance to make sense of confusing thoughts. As you start writing, you may find that your confusion begins to untangle itself through the process of putting words on the page.

Do your best not to respond to any of the questions in the way you would if your family, your friends or your work colleagues were watching. Unless you genuinely believe what you've written, keep challenging yourself by asking, 'Is this really true of me?'

You might also like to date your notes. It's often interesting to reflect back in a year or two to see if your thoughts have changed.

## PART ONE

# Connect with your true self

# ONE

# Finding your true self

*'If light is in your heart you will find your way home.'*

Rumi, 13th-century Persian poet, scholar and mystic

Before you were old enough to articulate your needs or understand your emotions, it's likely you had already been fed hundreds of messages that would influence your authentic character.

Across our childhood and teenage years, parents, siblings, teachers and friends share their opinions about the emotions we experience, the views we express, who we spend time with and the interests we have. Even the subtlest judgements imprint on our brains and before we are old enough to critically analyse whether there is truth or relevance in these judgements or whether they're inherently right for us, they become embedded in our subconscious mind.

It's not until much later, and often when we reach a crossroad or a crisis point in life, that we become aware that some of these messages have closed down parts of our authentic character. Messages designed to protect us or help us understand what was 'right' and 'wrong' in our family of origin, with our friends or within the context of our social group, have made us mould ourselves to fit other people's expectations.

During this process, the pure, authentic, creative and joyful spirit we were born with can become lost beneath layers of conforming behaviours.

Most of us still do have a sense of who we are – or at least, we have a sense when we're not being true to ourselves – but many of us have aspects of our personality that we have taken on because at some point in time, we believed this was expected of us.

The following chapters will help you connect with your true self. Once you've completed the exercises, you'll have a greater under-standing of your needs, your values, your strengths and the patterns of thinking that are keeping you from being your best self.

As you attune to your inner world, you'll start to become more aware in the outer world when you do things to please other people; when you stay silent but you really want to speak up; when you pretend you're confident instead of admitting you're vulnerable; when you compare yourself to other people or make life choices that look good on the outside but don't feel quite right on the inside.

We do these things often but we're sometimes unaware of how much they deplete our energy and diminish our sense of wholeness and happiness. Almost all our unhelpful life choices are related to judgement. When we're being overly self-critical, we judge our own and other people's lives and we measure ourselves against them.

It's likely you're most familiar with these feelings after spending time on social media. You scroll for a few minutes and see someone on an extravagant holiday or having fun with a group of friends and you notice a change in your energy. As you compare yourself, you feel diminished in some way. You forget about the positive aspects of your own life and you lose touch with your personal values.

This cycle of judging, comparing and competing leaves us feeling that there's always something to fix, to change or to achieve. However, our efforts to create lives that look perfect to others often lead to life choices that aren't genuinely fulfilling.

Most of us believe that the fundamental version of ourselves is flawed in some way. We hide our insecurities and our vulnerabilities to present a polished, well-put-together version of ourselves. We mask the aspects we're not proud of. We fear that when people *really get to know us*, they might turn away or reject us.

What I've learned in my work with clients and from experiences in my own life is that when we're not being really true to ourselves, it's difficult to build genuine connections and it's impossible to create a life where we feel grounded and whole and fulfilled.

This was certainly the case for Anastasia, who came to see me when she was in her mid-thirties. Growing up in a family with a lower income than many of her friends, Anastasia had always felt inferior in some way. She worked hard at uni and spent her twenties chasing well-paid marketing roles. Across every aspect of her life, she pushed herself to be perfect. She maintained a brutal schedule at the gym, met a high-achieving partner and they holidayed in beautiful places. Despite having everything she wanted and being all that she had ever aspired to be, when she came to see me she told me she felt entirely empty.

She had modelled her life around all the external factors that were missing in her childhood and along the way, she had lost clarity about who she was and what she wanted.

When we feel directionless or lost or dissatisfied with our lives, we often look at what we can change on the outside. A new job, a different partner, a bigger apartment, another degree, a health regime, a move overseas – we think we need something to fix our lives or find a way to make ourselves 'better'. We ask friends for their opinion, we talk to counsellors and coaches, we read books and ask Google and at the same time, we ignore the most important source of wisdom.

Our own internal guidance.

We don't take time to think about how we can *find our way home to ourselves*: that is, how we can reconnect with the experiences, the interests, the activities and the people who make us feel most real. How we can find a greater sense of inner peace, how we can cultivate self-acceptance, and how we can establish a balance between enjoying the here and now and moving forward in a meaningful way.

We all have our own ways of moving away from ourselves. We choose a career path because it's sensible. We chase status or money or power. In our efforts to make our lives look perfect to others, we hide our insecurities and fears – often even from ourselves.

Anastasia's underlying sense of not feeling good enough had made her ambitious, self-sufficient and emotionally reserved. Being protective of her feelings of vulnerability, she found it difficult to make genuine connections. A significant part of her emptiness stemmed from the feeling that she was completely alone. Despite fulfilling all the external measures of success that had seemed so important to her, Anastasia realised she had lost touch with some of her family's values of community, connection and kindness.

~

## Meaningful change begins on the inside

Before you begin to change your outer life, you need to know yourself well enough to be able to move beyond the thoughts, beliefs and behaviours that keep you repeating the same patterns that have made you unfulfilled in the first place.

Over the coming week, try to tune in when you're not being yourself. Check your energy levels after interacting with different people. When you're being true to yourself, you'll feel lighter and more energised afterwards; when you're not being real, you'll feel heavy or drained. With this first element of awareness, you can begin the journey of becoming truer to yourself.

~

# Are you in touch with your true self?

To get a sense of how connected you are with yourself, take the quiz below, giving yourself one point for every 'yes', half a point for each 'maybe' and zero for every 'no'. Total your score out of 20.

| QUIZ | SCORE |
|---|---|
| 1. I am aware of my personal values and as much as possible, I live in alignment with these most days. | |
| 2. While I value personal growth, I am mostly able to accept my imperfections. | |
| 3. I take care of my physical wellbeing in ways that feel nurturing and supportive to me. | |
| 4. I am aware of my body and notice when my muscles are tight if I'm feeling stressed. | |

| | |
|---|---|
| 5. I take care of my mental wellbeing, including reaching out for support when I feel I need it. | |
| 6. In most of my relationships, I feel accepted and appreciated for who I am. | |
| 7. For the most part, I feel that I am authentic and real when I'm with other people. | |
| 8. I practise being compassionate with myself. | |
| 9. I know my natural strengths and use these most days. | |
| 10. I gain personal satisfaction from the work that I do. | |
| 11. I have a few interests that I love and make time for. | |
| 12. I spend time reflecting on the things that are going well in my life. | |
| 13. My home environment feels peaceful and nurturing to me. | |
| 14. I have a sense of purpose in my life and know how to bring this to life in some way every day. | |
| 15. I feel part of something bigger than myself (for example, community, spirituality, a connection with nature). | |
| 16. I bring my awareness into the present moment, even if just briefly, on a regular basis. | |
| 17. I am aware of my habitual patterns of negative thinking. | |
| 18. I trust my intuition. | |
| 19. While I may not enjoy conflict, I'm able to speak up and voice my needs. | |
| 20. I know how to set boundaries and practise self-care. | |
| **SCORE** | **/20** |

## How did you score?

If you scored 15 or over, it's likely that you're connected with yourself and fairly content with who you are. You may still be interested in changing one or more of the areas where you've scored either half a point or a zero. It's possible that these could be affecting your overall life satisfaction.

If you scored between 7 and 15, there may be a few areas of your life you feel motivated to change. Rather than tackling everything at once, choose one (or at the most, two) areas you'd like to address as priorities and keep them in mind as you read through the following pages.

If your score is lower than 7, you'll probably find it helpful to have some support as you work through the process of change. A good friend or a supportive family member might be able to assist, but it can also be beneficial to work with someone who is unbiased, such as a psychologist, coach or counsellor. Speak to your GP about a mental health plan so you can access subsidised sessions with a psychologist.

## One small change

Once you've chosen the area you'd like to begin focusing on, be specific about the kind of change you'd like to see. Make a note of one small action step you can take in the coming week that will immediately move you in the direction of that change, even if it doesn't resolve the situation completely.

For example, if the exercises highlighted that you'd like to be more true to yourself, your commitment and action might be as follows:

| Commitment | Action |
| --- | --- |
| To be myself with my friends | *Catch myself when I'm changing my behaviour to try to fit in, and be more authentic instead.* |
|  |  |

# TWO

# Your life story

*'If I ever go looking for my heart's desire again, I won't look any further than my own backyard. Because if it isn't there, I never really lost it to begin with.'*
L. Frank Baum, *The Wonderful Wizard of Oz*

Telling stories in coaching or counselling sessions builds connection between the client and the coach/counsellor, which begins the process of healing. This is particularly evident where the professional is able to listen without interruption and to ask questions or offer validation in a way that makes the client feel that there's no judgement. Sharing your story with an empathic and caring listener helps you to know yourself well and it will also help you to understand how and why these events have shaped your life. If the listener is truly listening from the heart, the experience can make you feel seen and understood, which can alleviate the feelings of shame and isolation you may have experienced when you kept life events a secret.

I would begin my half-day sessions by asking my clients to share their story. Sometimes, after completing this exercise, a client would tell me they felt truly heard for the first time. As they listen to themselves, they begin to understand the relevance and the impact of their story on the way they perceive themselves and the choices they've made in their lives.

All of our stories matter. Regardless of our life circumstances or experiences, there are moments of beauty, pain, love, connection, heartbreak, guilt, shame, pride and wisdom in all of our lives. We encounter people who lift us and others who diminish us. There are all sorts of experiences from your past that will still be influencing you today.

How you interpret your life and how you tell your story to yourself (and others) has a profound effect on the person you become. Our stories give meaning to our existence and they also significantly shape our identity.

My client Jack recalled a life event that he'd completely forgotten about. Jack grew up in Kenya in the late 1950s. As he started to tell me his story, he remembered an incident that he'd never shared before, from around the time he was four years of age. He knew it was this early in his life because his younger brother had not yet been born.

Jack and his mother were out walking in their local neighbourhood when they encountered a group of young men hurriedly removing the wheels from a car. Jack could clearly recall sensing aggression and violence in that encounter and he had a vivid memory of his mother's fear. Jack realised as he spoke that this was one of a handful of memories from his early childhood that had given him the sense that the world was not a safe place.

He made the connection that an underlying anxiety was still playing out in his adult life, particularly when he felt that his decisions might impact the security of others. He remembered feeling somehow responsible for his mother's safety, even as a small child.

Just bringing his awareness to these thoughts helped Jack to interact with his fears differently. He was able to recognise that it was irrational to take responsibility for everyone else's safety and he also became aware of his inclination to exaggerate everyday worries and fears.

## What's your life story?

Using the following timeline, map out the most memorable and meaningful events in your life from the time you were born until now. A small caution before you begin – if you have experienced trauma in your past or if you have a niggling sense that opening the door on childhood memories might be unsettling for you, you may want to skip this exercise for now or at least stay away from any challenging or disturbing memories.

If you feel instinctively that it may be more helpful to share your story in a safe setting, reach out to a qualified therapist and ask them if you can work through this exercise verbally with their support.

If you have difficulty recalling your early years, begin by writing a paragraph or two in your journal about any aspects of the physical surroundings you can recall and write about how it felt to be in those surroundings.

As you begin to immerse yourself in your physical environment, it's likely you'll find that one memory triggers another.

| Age | Memories | Insights |
|---|---|---|
| 0–5 years: | | |
| 6–12 years: | | |
| 13–18 years: | | |
| 19–25 years: | | |
| 26–30 years: | | |
| 31–40 years: | | |
| 41–50 years: | | |
| 51–60 years: | | |
| 61+ years: | | |

## Share your story

Find a listener who is compassionate, kind and unlikely to judge you. Let them know that this exercise calls for them to listen for around one hour while you tell your life story. Keeping your storytelling time brief helps you to summarise events and stick to the facts, rather than getting overly caught up in the detail or drama of your story.

Again, if you have concerns that your story will raise traumatic memories, this exercise is best conducted with a psychologist, counsellor or coach.

Jot down any insights in your notebook or journal as you share your story.

## The benefits of telling your story

- Our stories can be the gateway to connection with other people, but equally, they help us really connect with our true selves.
- When we're able to look back at how we have overcome personal struggles, often we can see our own resilience.
- When you're able to tell your story in a factual way, you may find that you're better able to understand why people behaved as they did, making it easier to forgive yourself or others for past mistakes.
- Coming to terms with the events that have shaped your life can also help you find meaning from painful or difficult experiences.
- Your insights may help you to be more aware when you are unconsciously acting out patterns of behaviour that originated in younger years.

## Gathering insights

Spend some time now looking over your life story and gather any insights you have about yourself after telling your story. Think about how some events still influence your thinking patterns and behaviour today. As you reflect, do your best not to judge yourself or others – as best you can, simply note any insights from a place of impartiality.

## Your insights

. . . . . . . . . . . . . . . . . . . . . . . . . . . . . . . . . . . . . . . . . . . . . .

. . . . . . . . . . . . . . . . . . . . . . . . . . . . . . . . . . . . . . . . . . . . . .

. . . . . . . . . . . . . . . . . . . . . . . . . . . . . . . . . . . . . . . . . . . . . .

. . . . . . . . . . . . . . . . . . . . . . . . . . . . . . . . . . . . . . . . . . . . . .

. . . . . . . . . . . . . . . . . . . . . . . . . . . . . . . . . . . . . . . . . . . . . .

. . . . . . . . . . . . . . . . . . . . . . . . . . . . . . . . . . . . . . . . . . . . . .

. . . . . . . . . . . . . . . . . . . . . . . . . . . . . . . . . . . . . . . . . . . . . .

. . . . . . . . . . . . . . . . . . . . . . . . . . . . . . . . . . . . . . . . . . . . . .

. . . . . . . . . . . . . . . . . . . . . . . . . . . . . . . . . . . . . . . . . . . . . .

. . . . . . . . . . . . . . . . . . . . . . . . . . . . . . . . . . . . . . . . . . . . . .

. . . . . . . . . . . . . . . . . . . . . . . . . . . . . . . . . . . . . . . . . . . . . .

. . . . . . . . . . . . . . . . . . . . . . . . . . . . . . . . . . . . . . . . . . . . . .

. . . . . . . . . . . . . . . . . . . . . . . . . . . . . . . . . . . . . . . . . . . . . .

. . . . . . . . . . . . . . . . . . . . . . . . . . . . . . . . . . . . . . . . . . . . . .

. . . . . . . . . . . . . . . . . . . . . . . . . . . . . . . . . . . . . . . . . . . . . .

# THREE

# What are your needs?

*'We're only as needy as our unmet needs.'*

John Bowlby

All of us have a need for safety, love, acceptance, connection and a sense of purpose and belonging. We prioritise our needs differently in terms of how they've been met or not met as we grow up.

Understanding your needs will help you to better understand your emotions and your habitual behaviours, which are often what we use to make sure our needs are met. When our needs are satisfied, we feel a range of positive emotions (loving, confident, hopeful, joyful, peaceful) and our behavioural choices are more likely to be positive too.

When our needs aren't satisfied, we feel more negative emotions (sadness, anger, fear, frustration, tension) and we generally respond by either fixating on meeting the need at any cost, or denying the need altogether. Both of these options can lead to habits and behaviours that inhibit our emotional wellbeing and deny us the ability to live truly fulfilling lives.

~

My client Gemma had a long history of not having her needs met. Growing up with a narcissistic mother, Gemma felt that she had never really been understood, genuinely loved or accepted. Her mother's own need for love and acceptance (which Gemma later realised had never been met either), meant she used her children as a means of seeking approval. She dressed Gemma and her sister in matching outfits and insisted that they were always on their best behaviour. In her mother's presence, Gemma felt as though she only existed for her 'goodness'.

When she tried to talk to her mother about any concerns she had, her mother shut her down, turning the attention to her own problems. Gemma entered her teenage years with little self-worth and an inability to create genuine connections with people. Because she had never felt truly seen or understood, she sensed that something was inherently wrong with her.

Unaware that she was overly fixated on meeting her need for love and acceptance, Gemma spent almost a decade jumping from one unhappy partner relationship to the next. Her habit of people-pleasing meant she always reshaped herself to fit into her partner's world, changing her own interests, behaviours and even her dress sense in order to fit in. She had no sense at all of her authentic self.

When she came to see me, Gemma's partner had just left her and her self-esteem was low. We started by exploring her needs.

In order to find your way back to your true self, you need to understand your most deeply felt needs. Some will be needs that were well-met in your younger years; others will be needs you have pushed aside or denied.

In Gemma's case, for example, although she'd never had trouble finding partners, she had always found it difficult to find like-minded friends. Because she had no sense of her true self and was always adapting herself to fit in, she never felt fully accepted. As a result, she kept most of her friends at arms-length. In her early adult years, she stopped trying to get close to friends and instead became overly self-sufficient in all relationships other than the one with her partner.

We worked together to help Gemma understand her true needs. While she knew her need for *acceptance* was strong, she realised she needed to work on the need for *authenticity* first. As Gemma started to know herself better, she realised she could interact with everyone, including herself, very differently.

When we are able to accept that many needs are universal, we usually find we can be less critical of ourselves for having these needs. When we come to recognise how our needs weren't well met in our younger years, we can cultivate a kinder, more positive relationship with ourselves and we begin to take responsibility for having our needs met in more helpful ways.

## Identifying your needs

Look over the following table and identify the most pressing psychological needs in your life. Try to do this quickly and intuitively, rather than overthinking it. Select as many areas of need as you like and if there's a need you're aware of that's not listed below, add it in your journal. As you cast your eyes across the list, you may also become aware of other external needs that are not being met. You may like to note those down too. Once you have drafted your list, use the scoring system below to note how well your needs are currently being met.

0 = not at all  1 = rarely  2 = sometimes  3 = mostly  4 = almost always  5 = always

| Connection | | Honesty | | Humour | |
|---|---|---|---|---|---|
| Closeness | | Living ethically | | Sense of community | |
| Belonging | | Safety | | Sense of purpose | |
| Affection | | Challenge | | Sensuality | |
| Nurturing | | Order | | Learning | |
| Respect | | Communication | | Inclusion | |
| To feel understood | | Touch | | Spirituality | |
| To feel seen | | Choice | | Support | |
| Trust | | Spontaneity | | Independence | |
| Autonomy | | Meaning | | Tranquillity | |
| Stability | | Creativity | | Space | |
| Freedom | | Acceptance | | Intimacy | |
| Authenticity | | Equality | | Agency | |
| Contribution | | Appreciation | | Empathy | |

# What makes you 'needy'?

When an enduring emotional closeness was missing or unpredictable in childhood, sometimes our need for connection can leave us feeling fearful or helpless or overly dependent upon others.

Neediness is probably best described as an unhealthy craving for connection – a feeling that leaves us clingy and vulnerable and afraid of rejection. Because of this fear, you might find yourself being overly sensitive to changes in the mood or behaviour of the person you're trying to get close to. The resulting anxiety makes you less likely to clearly communicate your needs and your anxious behaviour has the potential to drive people away from you.

## Overcoming 'neediness'

- Become more aware of how you interact in your relationships. If you notice a 'neediness' in you, tune in to the emotions that are present.
- Take a few breaths and do your best to calm your anxiety.
- Spend some time journalling about your feelings – be curious about where they've come from.
- Avoid a passive communication style and instead, be open about your needs. Communicate your needs to the people closest to you using 'I' statements, for example, 'I would love it if we could spend time together this weekend.'
- Learn to offer yourself reassurance. Validate your feelings and remind yourself that you can cope, even when all your needs are not met.
- Become more comfortable spending time on your own.
- Look for relationships where the other person demonstrates a desire to spend time with you too.

# Meeting your needs in a healthy way

Choose one need from the table on page 19 that you feel is not currently being met. Note one small action step you can take this week to have this need met more effectively and make a point of taking that step, ideally in the next few days.

If you've chosen a need that hasn't been met for a long time (or maybe forever), it's possible that identifying the need may also bring up some sadness, or in extreme cases, even grief. You may want to work your way through these emotions with a professional.

If your needs bring up slightly painful but manageable emotions, jump ahead to the chapter on self-compassion (page 115) and implement some of these practices right away.

Here's an example:

**My need:** *To feel a sense of belonging.*

**How I sabotage this need:** *I don't let people get close to me because I worry that I'll get hurt.*

**A healthy way to meet this need:** *I'll invite my new work colleague for coffee because I sense that we might have some common interests.*

. . . . . . . . . . . . . . . . . . . . . . . . . . . . . . . . . . . . . . . . . . . . . . .
. . . . . . . . . . . . . . . . . . . . . . . . . . . . . . . . . . . . . . . . . . . . . . .
. . . . . . . . . . . . . . . . . . . . . . . . . . . . . . . . . . . . . . . . . . . . . . .
. . . . . . . . . . . . . . . . . . . . . . . . . . . . . . . . . . . . . . . . . . . . . . .
. . . . . . . . . . . . . . . . . . . . . . . . . . . . . . . . . . . . . . . . . . . . . . .
. . . . . . . . . . . . . . . . . . . . . . . . . . . . . . . . . . . . . . . . . . . . . . .
. . . . . . . . . . . . . . . . . . . . . . . . . . . . . . . . . . . . . . . . . . . . . . .
. . . . . . . . . . . . . . . . . . . . . . . . . . . . . . . . . . . . . . . . . . . . . . .
. . . . . . . . . . . . . . . . . . . . . . . . . . . . . . . . . . . . . . . . . . . . . . .

# FOUR

# Identify your values

*'Let yourself be silently drawn by the strange pull of what you really love.*
*It will not lead you astray.'*
Rumi, 13th-century Persian poet, scholar and mystic

One of the greatest regrets people express at the end of their lives is not living in a way that was true for them. In other words, not being aligned with their personal values. Your values are the guiding principles that influence how you live your life and how you behave as a person. They might also be described as *your heart's deepest desires* or *the measures by which you determine whether your life is well lived.*

Ideally, we'll use our values to guide our life choices in the present moment, regardless of the circumstances or situations we find ourselves in. Even when we're not achieving our goals, we can be true to our values every day. While some values will remain with us forever, it's also likely that others will change in relation to our life circumstances.

When we identify our values, we can use them in a range of different ways.

**Your values can:**

- Guide your behaviour in everyday life.
- Provide a measure against which you benchmark your life choices.
- Help you understand where and why you feel compromised in life.
- Steer you onto a life path that feels inherently right for you.
- Help you define your life purpose.

Once you have identified your values, they can influence decision-making in all areas of your life. They'll help you determine how you want to live and work; they will influence your behaviour; they'll play a part in helping you choose who you spend time with; and it's likely that they'll have an impact on how you take care of your physical and mental wellbeing. They may also have an effect on how you earn and spend money; how you make use of your leisure time; and they will shape your environmental, social and political beliefs.

# When your values differ from those of your family

Some values, like character traits, appear to be with us right from the moment we enter the world. I've met clients who tell me that, from as early as they can remember, they felt an instinctive desire to express 'kindness', despite it not being an obvious value in their family of origin.

Some say they felt drawn to the value of 'creativity', even though no one around them was overtly creative. Others display a natural inclination towards 'courage' when it wasn't something they'd witnessed often.

When our personal values are a close match for those of our family, we generally experience a sense of validation and belonging as we grow up. But when our values differ from those closest to us, we might feel conflicted or inclined to compromise values we may otherwise hold most dear.

# Know your true values

When you know and can express your true personal values, you're more likely to make choices that feel authentic and inherently right for you. Your values can help direct you to a life that is fulfilling, even before you achieve your most important goals.

Consider your VALUES as the guiding principles that you can align with at all times – in your relationships, in the way you conduct yourself, in your workplace and in relation to the world. Regardless of your external circumstances, your values can act as an inner compass that will keep you on track as you navigate life's more complex decisions.

## Identify your personal values

Complete the following steps to help you identify your personal values. You may want to note and date your responses in your journal so that you can review them in a few months.

### 1. Peak experiences

In 1964 Abraham Maslow coined the term 'peak experience' to denote sudden feelings of intense wellbeing that fill us with wonder and awe. He described a peak experience as:

> *Feelings of limitless horizons opening up to the vision.*
> *The feeling of being simultaneously more powerful and also*

*more helpless than one ever was before. The feeling of ecstasy
and wonder and awe. The loss of placement in time and
space with, finally, the conviction that something extremely
important and valuable had happened, so that the subject was
to some extent transformed and strengthened even in his daily
life by such experiences.*

Peak experiences can help us to gain a clear sense of what matters most in our lives and they're an excellent way to connect us with our values. They are often moments when we feel fully awake or alive. Sometimes they feel wonderful and at other times they happen during periods of great sadness. People often say that either during or after such experiences they notice a shift in the way they think or how they live.

When we recall our positive peak experiences, we can often identify the values that were present and engaged. One of my most memorable peak moments occurred when Chris and I spent a weekend away together on the east coast of Tasmania when our girls were little. We woke up early to take photographs while the morning was clear and still. We walked to a pebbly beach that overlooked The Hazards mountain range and I took a moment to sit by the water and watch the sun rise while Chris was taking photos. As I sat, I became aware of the warmth of the sun on my skin and the sound of the pebbles rolling with the movement of the water. I was aware of an appreciation for the beauty of nature, a feeling of connection with Chris and a deep sense of inner peace. In that moment, I was engaging my values of aesthetic appreciation, connection and inner harmony.

We can make the same links when we recall emotionally challenging peak moments, by recognising the values that were compromised or conflicted. When we experience emotional hurt or we feel confronted by someone's dishonesty for example, we might discover that our values of kindness or integrity have been compromised.

Spend some time thinking about the moments in your life when emotion was heightened. Describe where you were, who you were with and what you were doing in as much detail as possible.

Don't be surprised if initially your mind goes blank when you try to recall peak experiences. It can take some time to remember them. If you still find it difficult after a few hours, you may find it helpful to get into a relaxed state by meditating before you begin.

As you write about your peak experience, also reflect on which values you were engaging or which values were compromised during the experience.

. . . . . . . . . . . . . . . . . . . . . . . . . . . . . . . . . . . . . . . . . . . . . . . . . . . . . . .

. . . . . . . . . . . . . . . . . . . . . . . . . . . . . . . . . . . . . . . . . . . . . . . . . . . . . .

. . . . . . . . . . . . . . . . . . . . . . . . . . . . . . . . . . . . . . . . . . . . . . . . . . . . . .

. . . . . . . . . . . . . . . . . . . . . . . . . . . . . . . . . . . . . . . . . . . . . . . . . . . . . .

. . . . . . . . . . . . . . . . . . . . . . . . . . . . . . . . . . . . . . . . . . . . . . . . . . . . . . .

. . . . . . . . . . . . . . . . . . . . . . . . . . . . . . . . . . . . . . . . . . . . . . . . . . . . . .

## 2. Be guided by your role models

Think of a few people you admire or respect greatly and consider the values they embody. For example, a friend who always has something positive to say about others might have values of optimism or kindness. A manager who is intelligent and unassuming might have values of wisdom and humility.

Make a note of these role models and the values you would love to emulate.

. . . . . . . . . . . . . . . . . . . . . . . . . . . . . . . . . . . . . . . . . . . . . . . .

. . . . . . . . . . . . . . . . . . . . . . . . . . . . . . . . . . . . . . . . . . . . . . . .

. . . . . . . . . . . . . . . . . . . . . . . . . . . . . . . . . . . . . . . . . . . . . . . .

. . . . . . . . . . . . . . . . . . . . . . . . . . . . . . . . . . . . . . . . . . . . . . . .

. . . . . . . . . . . . . . . . . . . . . . . . . . . . . . . . . . . . . . . . . . . . . . . .

. . . . . . . . . . . . . . . . . . . . . . . . . . . . . . . . . . . . . . . . . . . . . . . .

### 3. When are you most depleted or energised?

My client Laura discovered a clash of values when she spent time socialising with some of her workmates. The small group of colleagues who invited her to join them for lunch enjoyed gossiping about team members who weren't present. Laura left those lunches feeling drained and uncomfortable.

She was conflicted because for the most part, she enjoyed the company of her colleagues but she came to realise that her values of loyalty and integrity were compromised when she heard them speaking unkindly about others.

My client Sally joined a new friend in a ceramics class after work and even when the class ran over time and she had a late night, she felt mentally stimulated and energised. Sally discovered how much enjoyment she gained from engaging her values of creativity and connection.

Think back across the past week and try to identify times when you were noticeably drained or energised. Which values were being compromised or engaged?

. . . . . . . . . . . . . . . . . . . . . . . . . . . . . . . . . . . . . . . . . . . . . . . .

. . . . . . . . . . . . . . . . . . . . . . . . . . . . . . . . . . . . . . . . . . . . . . . .

. . . . . . . . . . . . . . . . . . . . . . . . . . . . . . . . . . . . . . . . . . . . . . .
. . . . . . . . . . . . . . . . . . . . . . . . . . . . . . . . . . . . . . . . . . . . . . .
. . . . . . . . . . . . . . . . . . . . . . . . . . . . . . . . . . . . . . . . . . . . . . .

## 4. Choose your values from the list

1. Using the list on page 29, circle the values that feel important to you.

2. For each value, write a sentence or two about how this value might be expressed in your life. For example the value of connection to you may mean *to be open and expressive with my partner; to spend time with my two closest friends; to stay in regular touch with my parents and brother; to feel part of my community by participating in art classes and to connect with myself during my daily yoga practice.*

3. You may also like to note the specific ways these values have benefited you in the past and consider what your life might have been like without these values.

## 5. Group your values

Create between three and five 'categories' and group your values into these categories as best you can. For example, one category might include the values of *belonging, connection and friendship* and another *autonomy, achievement, economic security and work ethic.*

Once you've grouped your values, choose one word that best represents what each value group means to you. For example, the first example above might be called *Belonging* and the second, *Achievement.*

Try to memorise your values categories and when you have an important decision to make, benchmark that against your values. Will the action move you closer or further away from given values?

# Values list

| | | | |
|---|---|---|---|
| Abundance | Economic | Humility | Pleasure |
| Acceptance |   security | Humour | Popularity |
| Achievement | Empathy | Inclusiveness | Prosperity |
| Adventure | Encouragement | Independence | Purpose |
| Advocacy | Environment | Inner harmony | Recognition |
| Aesthetic | Equality | Innovation | Resilience |
| Affection | Ethics | Integrity | Safety |
| Appreciation | Excellence | Intellect | Security |
| Autonomy | Excitement | Joy | Self-care |
| Balance | Fairness | Justice | Sensuality |
| Belonging | Fame | Kindness | Serenity |
| Boldness | Family | Knowledge | Simplicity |
| Calmness | Flexibility | Leadership | Social |
| Caring | Forgiveness | Learning |   engagement |
| Challenge | Freedom | Love | Solitude |
| Cheerfulness | Friendship | Loyalty | Spirituality |
| Collaboration | Fun | Meaning | Status |
| Community | Generosity | Mindfulness | Time freedom |
| Compassion | Grace | Open-mindedness | Tolerance |
| Competition | Gratitude | Optimism | Tradition |
| Connection | Growth | Order | Tranquillity |
| Contribution | Harmony | Peace | Trust |
| Courage | Health | Persistence | Wealth |
| Creativity | Helping others | Personal | Wisdom |
| Curiosity | Honesty |   development | Work ethic |
| | Humanitarianism | Playfulness | |

My client, Elena, found it difficult to choose her values when we first worked through this exercise.

Growing up, hard work was a core value in Elena's family. As the first child of immigrant parents, from the age of nine Elena had taken care of her two younger siblings while her parents worked long hours in the family business. There was little time for leisure for any of the family members and whenever Elena felt the desire to engage in an activity purely for the joy of it, her overriding emotion was guilt.

Like many of my clients, Elena pushed aside what she perceived to be her less practical values of 'creativity' and 'inner harmony' and instead, she emphasised 'work ethic', 'recognition' and 'persistence'. These values were familiar and comfortable and she knew how to align them with her high-pressure corporate finance role.

When Elena came to see me, she felt depleted by her never-ending task list and by the pressure that she put herself under to work long hours, with little time for rest.

Completing the values exercise was initially uncomfortable for Elena. She was torn between her long-held family values and a desire to bring her other personal values to life.

In the end, Elena made a choice to maintain the family values that related to hard work but she also included 'inner harmony' and 'creativity' in her list, knowing that making room for these would help her to create more balance in her life.

## How aligned with your values are you?

Reflect back on your top values and consider how aligned you are with each of them.

Give yourself a score out of 10 – with 10 being, 'I am completely aligned with this value and a score of 1 being, 'I'm not honouring this value at all'.

Once you have identified your scores, consider a few small action steps to take in the coming week to become more aligned with your values. For example, if you're like Elena and one of your top values is 'inner harmony', but you don't currently give yourself time to rest, one action step might be 'to pause before agreeing to any new commitments in the coming week' or 'to set aside time on Sunday afternoon for self-care'.

| Value | Score | Ideas / action steps |
|---|---|---|
| e.g. Inner harmony | 5/10 | Pause before agreeing to new commitments. Set aside Sunday afternoon to rest. |
| 1 | | |
| 2 | | |
| 3 | | |
| 4 | | |
| 5 | | |

The key to embracing a values-led life is to check in with your values on a regular basis. While it's unlikely that you'll be perfectly aligned with every value at all times, revisiting your list on a regular basis will help you to see where you're overextending yourself or neglecting important aspects of your life.

Be mindful also that when you make an adjustment in one values area, it may impact another. For example, increasing 'inner harmony' may reduce your alignment with 'achievement'.

Over time, you'll come to recognise that this is an exercise in ongoing recalibration.

# Using your values in your everyday life

Now that you have clarity about your personal values, use them as the cornerstone for all your life decisions.

1. Memorise your values categories and benchmark any important decisions against them. Ask yourself, 'Does this decision align with my top values or will it move me further away?'

2. On any given day, choose one value to highlight. As you go about your usual activities, check in and see if you're engaging with life in a way that feels aligned.

3. Next time you find yourself feeling discontent, choose one simple action step that will align you more closely with one of your values. For example, when you become aware that you're not feeling as close to your partner and one of your values is 'connection', make a commitment to share your feelings more openly.

4. Be respectful of the fact that the people in your life will have their own values and they may differ from yours. If you can find a way to agree on a couple of values, you may find this gives you an opportunity for connection.

5. Acknowledge that you while you may not always be able to align with all your values, having clarity about them can change your life.

# FIVE

# Discover your strengths

*'Nothing can dim the light which shines from within.'*

Maya Angelou

Traditionally, the focus of therapy was to help people understand and resolve their problems. Two decades ago, a group of psychologists recognised that this emphasis did not adequately take into account what is already good within us or what makes our lives worth living. In the late 1990s, in the early days of the positive psychology movement, Martin Seligman and his colleagues began to research human flourishing. One aspect of this work was to study the human virtues and strengths that allow individuals to flourish.

Positive psychology suggests that identifying and engaging your strengths on a regular basis not only contributes to your wellbeing but also enhances your sense of fulfilment in life.

In his book *Authentic Happiness*, Seligman identified three key elements of life that contribute to positive mental health and wellbeing. These are:

1. The Pleasant Life (which is made up of pleasant emotions and experiences).
2. The Engaged Life (where you regularly engage your strengths and move into the state of 'flow').
3. The Meaningful Life (where you use your strengths to contribute to something bigger than you).

Seligman suggests that a good life constitutes engaging all three areas. When we immerse ourselves in the latter two 'lives' our focus is on redesigning our activities so that we use our highest strengths on a regular basis. We can do this in our workplaces, in our relationships, in the way we parent our children and in our leisure activities.

Seligman's team identified six human virtues (or qualities of good human conduct) that transcend cultural, religious, philosophical and generational boundaries. Their work led them to name 24 strengths that sit beneath these virtues that are considered to reflect the essence of all human character.

When an individual's top strengths are engaged, they are most likely to move into the state of 'flow'– a state of being that is outlined in detail by Hungarian psychologist Mihaly Csikszentmihalyi, in his book, *Flow: The Psychology of Optimal Experience.*

Csikszentmihalyi describes the state of flow as being characterised by a few key elements. When you're in a state of flow you lose all sense of time and self-consciousness. You might even feel that you lose yourself in the task you're engaged in. Your focus and your concentration level are narrowed – you are completely immersed in the activity and the activity itself provides you with a degree of direct feedback. In flow, there's a sense of balance between the level of difficulty of the task and the level of your ability to complete that task.

In other words, the activity is challenging enough to keep you stimulated but a close enough match to your expertise that you won't be totally frustrated. In a state of flow, you feel a degree of personal control over your situation and there's an intrinsic sense of reward. You are completely absorbed by and focused on your task – and this can be the case even if only several of the elements outlined above are present.

## Being in flow means being yourself

Mihaly Csikszentmihalyi may have been the first Westerner to describe the concept of 'flow', but Eastern religions such as Buddhism and Taoism have made use of this principle as a means of personal and spiritual development for many years. While it's not the same as mindfulness, the state of flow brings you fully into the present moment – a state that many researchers believe to be an important contributing factor to well-being, and which requires you to be completely yourself.

By getting to know your unique strengths and finding ways to engage in activities where you use those strengths, you'll find yourself more regularly in this 'flow' state, which can lead you to a deeper sense of fulfilment in life. When we are in such a state, we are always being true to ourselves, and this is where we often find that our energy and zest for life is restored.

Most of us take our natural strengths for granted. We live with them every day and because we're so close to them, we don't recognise that these strengths are unique gifts that others don't always have.

We are also generally humble beings – we're more inclined to downplay our strengths than to honour them. When we assume that everyone has our strengths, we devalue our own uniqueness.

When we are able to embrace this uniqueness and explore how we can use our natural strengths every day, our lives become significantly richer.

## What are your strengths?

There are several ways to discover your strengths. The first is to visit the VIA Signature Strengths website (https://www.viacharacter.org/) to complete a free survey that is offered online by the founders of positive psychology. The test takes around 15 minutes to complete, resulting in a ranking of all 24 strengths. Your 'signature strengths' are considered to be the top-ranked strengths and those that best describe the positive aspects of your personality. When you engage these strengths, it's likely you'll feel energised and motivated.

Another option to help you identify your strengths is to reach out to at least five friends or family members and ask them what they believe to be your most dominant character strengths.

# Positive psychology virtues and strengths

| WISDOM | |
|---|---|
| **Creativity** | Artistic achievement; generating ideas; finding novel ways to do things. |
| **Curiosity** | An interest in learning; meeting new people; visiting new places; having many interest areas; asking lots of questions; being open-minded; exploring; discovering. |
| **Judgement** | Critical thinking; open-minded thinking; being willing to listen to all points of view; weighing all evidence fairly; not jumping to conclusions. |
| **Love of learning** | Learning on your own or through formal education; systematically building on your body of knowledge; mastering new knowledge; being eager to share what is learned. |
| **Perspective/ wisdom** | High level of knowledge; insightful beyond the facts; can offer wise counsel to others; capacity to explain the reasons 'why' to others. |
| **COURAGE** | |
| **Bravery** | Speaking up for what is right (even when unpopular); choosing to act on values and principles; includes physical bravery (but not limited to this). |
| **Perseverance** | Finishing what you start; working through obstacles; generally resilient. |
| **Honesty** | Being aligned with personal values; taking responsibility for your feelings and behaviours; being honest and ethical; having a high level of integrity. |
| **Zest** | Approaching life with vigour; living life as an adventure; not doing things half-heartedly. |
| **HUMANITY** | |
| **Love** | Valuing close relationships; the capacity to love and be loved; expressing love through deeds, words and affection. |
| **Kindness/ generosity** | Doing kind deeds for others; helping; taking care of others; being generous; nurturing. |
| **Social intelligence** | Fitting in to social settings; understanding motives and feelings of others and self. |

| JUSTICE | |
|---|---|
| Teamwork | Working well as part of a group; doing your share; staying loyal to the group. |
| Fairness | Treating others equally; giving everyone a chance; belief in justice. |
| Leadership | Encouraging and inspiring others while maintaining good relationships with them. |
| **TEMPERANCE** | |
| Forgiveness | Forgiving others; giving people a second chance; not holding grudges. |
| Humility | Letting your accomplishments speak for themselves; not believing you are anything special. |
| Prudence | Being careful with choices; not taking undue risks. |
| Self-regulation | Being disciplined; controlling one's appetites; regulating what one feels and does. |
| **TRANSCENDENCE** | |
| Appreciation of beauty and excellence | Appreciating beauty in nature; living with a sense of awe; recognising excellence in all areas of life; pursuing wonder. |
| Hope | Expecting the best in the future and working towards it; believing in a good future. |
| Gratitude | Counting one's blessings; taking time to feel thankful; being aware when good things happen. |
| Humour | Seeing the lighter side; making others laugh; being playful; not taking yourself too seriously. |
| Spirituality | Having a sense of connection with something bigger; pursuing deeper meaning in life. |

# Your top strengths

Review the strengths in the table above and make a note of any that you feel come naturally to you. You might like to asterisk any that you'd like to engage more frequently. Now note your top ten strengths on page 39 or in your journal.

1. . . . . . . . . . . . . . . . . . . . . . .     6. . . . . . . . . . . . . . . . . . . . .

2. . . . . . . . . . . . . . . . . . . . .     7. . . . . . . . . . . . . . . . . . . . . . .

3. . . . . . . . . . . . . . . . . . . . . .     8. . . . . . . . . . . . . . . . . . . . . .

4. . . . . . . . . . . . . . . . . . . . .     9. . . . . . . . . . . . . . . . . . . . . .

5. . . . . . . . . . . . . . . . . . . . .     10 . . . . . . . . . . . . . . . . . . . . .

## How can you use your strengths?

1. Reviewing your strengths above, write a paragraph or two in your journal about how you currently use these strengths at work and in your personal life.

2. If you discover one or two strengths that you're not engaging often, think of ways to bring these strengths to life.

3. If you find that you have an inclination to *overuse* a particular strength (which can actually be draining), make a note of how you can downplay it.

4. Looking at your top ten strengths, ask yourself whether any of these criteria apply:
   • Do you feel a sense of ownership of the strength? (Does it feel like the 'real you'?)
   • Can you identify any new ways to engage this strength?
   • Do you feel invigorated while using the strength (rather than exhausted)?
   • Do you have personal projects that utilise this strength?

5. Now look back at the strengths that *didn't make it to your list*. These may be attributes you simply don't enjoy using but there's a chance you consider one or more of these, to be *weaknesses*. Can you avoid using these altogether? Are there some that you

need to build up, in order to feel more fulfilled or energised? Or are there others you can simply let go of?

～

I worked with Lorenzo over 15 years ago now but his story has stayed with me since. In his preparatory paperwork, he noted that at 45, his secret passion was to be a rock star. Somehow, he'd found himself light years away from his dream and was working in a role as a technical writer. It was no surprise he wasn't content.

Lorenzo completed the strengths survey and we discovered that his top strength was 'appreciation of beauty and excellence'. This strength wasn't being utilised at all while he worked in front of a computer screen every day writing in technical language. His other strengths of 'humour', 'social intelligence', 'gratitude' and 'creativity' were rarely engaged because he worked from home and seldom interacted with other people.

We tackled the beauty and excellence strength first. Lorenzo decided to change his work environment so it felt more physically appealing. He cleared away clutter and added travel photos to the wall behind his desk and a few house plants to his home office. He was surprised at how such a small change made him immediately happier to be at his desk.

Next, we looked at how Lorenzo could shape his day so that he had more time to connect with people so he could use his strengths of humour and social intelligence. When it wasn't possible for him to catch up with colleagues (many worked interstate), he caught up with friends for coffee or a drink a couple of times each week. Lorenzo found it easy to bring his gratitude strength to life by thinking about three things he was grateful for every morning.

Finally, we tackled the strength of creativity. While he recognised it was probably too late to fulfil his rock star dreams, Lorenzo organised weekly guitar lessons and almost a year later, had a regular jamming session with a few other musicians.

# SIX

# Uncover your patterns of thinking

*'The words you speak become the house you live in.'*

Hafiz, 14th century Persian poet

Our habitual patterns of negative thinking usually have their roots in childhood. When our needs for security, empathy, love and acceptance were not adequately met as children, we subconsciously believe this is through some fault of our own. Negative thinking styles are one way we attempt to *fix ourselves* so we'll be more deserving of loving.

How we aim to meet our needs is influenced by our temperament. One child in a family with overly critical parents might do their best to behave perfectly while another may give up on achieving and become rebellious and defiant. Another with unavailable or unloving parents might become fiercely independent while their sibling might fixate on the fact that they're unlovable and go through life confirming this belief by choosing partners who are unavailable.

Often these negative patterns of thinking have become habitual by the time we enter adulthood. While they provide us with a sense of certainty and control by helping us to recreate the conditions of childhood, they're also the same habits that prevent us from having our genuine needs fulfilled. For the most part, they're unhelpful and self-limiting and once they are established, we have a tendency to repeat them over and over.

If we can become aware of these often hidden or unconscious patterns, we can use this awareness to slowly transform our inner and outer experience. Understanding and modifying our negative patterns of thinking has the power to significantly improve our lives.

While almost all our negative thought patterns fall into several main categories, there are often subtle differences in the way we apply such thoughts to ourselves. The lists on pages 45–7 will act as an introduction by helping you to recognise how you typically interact with yourself. You'll read more about how to reframe negative thoughts in Chapter 16 (page 145).

When Lucinda and I first spoke about her desire to become a more confident speaker, she recounted an incident from her childhood. Naturally introverted, Lucinda grew up with outgoing, confident parents. Her younger brother was gregarious and rebellious from an early age, and Lucinda had taken the position of the quiet, unassuming one in her family. At school, she avoided conflict and while she was intelligent enough to answer questions in class, for the most part she kept her hand by her side when the teacher asked for responses. She had a belief that she had nothing valuable to add in group settings.

In her last year of primary school, feeling liked by her teacher and more comfortable with her friendship group, Lucinda raised her hand in an English class to answer a question, and her response was ridiculed by a group of boys. Humiliated and embarrassed, Lucinda believed she had confirmation that her earlier assumption was right and since that time, she had stayed quiet in most group settings.

As we spoke, Lucinda identified her habitual pattern of thinking. She told herself she wasn't as confident, as articulate or as outgoing as other people, and noted her preference to stay out of the limelight. When she did find herself in a situation where she was asked to speak to a group – in a meeting setting at work, for example – Lucinda did her best to avoid having to respond.

Without being conscious that she was doing it, Lucinda was confirming her belief that she lacked confidence and had nothing interesting to add when asked to speak in a group setting.

## What are your patterns of thinking?

As you read through the following lists, make a note in your journal of any of these thoughts you're aware of, and also note any variations that are unique to you.

If your instinct tells you that you're not actively tuned in to your patterns of thinking, pause from time to time during the coming week and check in to see how you're feeling. When you become aware of less positive emotions, scan through the list and see if there's one thinking style that might have impacted your mood.

## Feeling less than others

- I'm not good enough
- I should be different from what I am
- I'm not as . . . as other people (e.g. confident, witty, articulate, gregarious, outgoing)
- I 'should' . . . (e.g. exercise more, eat better, be funnier, be smarter, prettier, thinner)
- I'm a fraud or an imposter
- I'm useless
- I could never . . . (something you want to do in your life)
- I need to always put others first

**How this influences my behaviour:**

. . . . . . . . . . . . . . . . . . . . . . . . . . . . . . . . . . . . . . . . . . . . . . . . . . . . . . . . .

. . . . . . . . . . . . . . . . . . . . . . . . . . . . . . . . . . . . . . . . . . . . . . . . . . . . . . . . .

. . . . . . . . . . . . . . . . . . . . . . . . . . . . . . . . . . . . . . . . . . . . . . . . . . . . . . . . .

## Feeling different from others

- I'm not like other people
- I don't fit in
- I'm an outsider
- I don't belong
- I'm too sensitive

**How this influences my behaviour:**

. . . . . . . . . . . . . . . . . . . . . . . . . . . . . . . . . . . . . . . . . . . . . . . . . . . . . . . . .

. . . . . . . . . . . . . . . . . . . . . . . . . . . . . . . . . . . . . . . . . . . . . . . . . . . . . . . . .

. . . . . . . . . . . . . . . . . . . . . . . . . . . . . . . . . . . . . . . . . . . . . . . . . . . . . . . . .

## Seeking approval

- I need to be liked by everyone
- I should always be a good person
- I can't say no
- I should never get angry

**How this influences my behaviour:**

. . . . . . . . . . . . . . . . . . . . . . . . . . . . . . . . . . . . . . . . . . . . . . . .

. . . . . . . . . . . . . . . . . . . . . . . . . . . . . . . . . . . . . . . . . . . . . . . .

. . . . . . . . . . . . . . . . . . . . . . . . . . . . . . . . . . . . . . . . . . . . . . . .

## Feeling fearful

- I'm not brave enough
- I'm not ready yet
- I'd rather choose the safe option
- I'm waiting for permission
- I don't know where to start
- I might fail
- I don't have the skills
- It will take a lot of time
- What will other people think?
- I'm going to get hurt
- I'd better not cause conflict

**How this influences my behaviour:**

. . . . . . . . . . . . . . . . . . . . . . . . . . . . . . . . . . . . . . . . . . . . . . . .

. . . . . . . . . . . . . . . . . . . . . . . . . . . . . . . . . . . . . . . . . . . . . . . .

. . . . . . . . . . . . . . . . . . . . . . . . . . . . . . . . . . . . . . . . . . . . . . . .

## Too much humility

- I shouldn't shine too brightly
- It's wrong to want more
- I should have to work really hard

**How this influences my behaviour:**

. . . . . . . . . . . . . . . . . . . . . . . . . . . . . . . . . . . . . . . . . . . . . . . . .

. . . . . . . . . . . . . . . . . . . . . . . . . . . . . . . . . . . . . . . . . . . . . . . . .

. . . . . . . . . . . . . . . . . . . . . . . . . . . . . . . . . . . . . . . . . . . . . . . . .

## Too much independence

- I should be able to do it all on my own
- It's wrong to ask for help
- I need to work harder
- I need to adhere to a strict routine
- No one will be there for me so I need to rely on myself

**How this influences my behaviour:**

. . . . . . . . . . . . . . . . . . . . . . . . . . . . . . . . . . . . . . . . . . . . . . . . .

. . . . . . . . . . . . . . . . . . . . . . . . . . . . . . . . . . . . . . . . . . . . . . . . .

. . . . . . . . . . . . . . . . . . . . . . . . . . . . . . . . . . . . . . . . . . . . . . . . .

## Putting everyone else first

- I want to do the right thing by other people
- My needs don't matter
- There's no space for me
- Being creative is indulgent
- I'm not contributing enough
- I need to be more generous
- I'm being selfish if I meet my own needs

**How this influences my behaviour:**

. . . . . . . . . . . . . . . . . . . . . . . . . . . . . . . . . . . . . . . . . . . . . . . . .

. . . . . . . . . . . . . . . . . . . . . . . . . . . . . . . . . . . . . . . . . . . . . . . . .

. . . . . . . . . . . . . . . . . . . . . . . . . . . . . . . . . . . . . . . . . . . . . . . . .

## Feelings of negativity or pessimism

• It won't work

• It's not worth trying

• It will be too hard

• I don't have the motivation

**How this influences my behaviour:**

. . . . . . . . . . . . . . . . . . . . . . . . . . . . . . . . . . . . . . . . . . . . . . . . .

. . . . . . . . . . . . . . . . . . . . . . . . . . . . . . . . . . . . . . . . . . . . . . . . .

. . . . . . . . . . . . . . . . . . . . . . . . . . . . . . . . . . . . . . . . . . . . . . . . .

# Bringing awareness to your thoughts

1. Over the coming week, try to catch yourself as you notice one of your habitual negative thoughts. Observe how those thoughts influence your behaviour.

2. Consider how this pattern of thinking is playing out in all the different areas of your life. Are there elements of your childhood you're unconsciously trying to recreate? How does the thought limit you in achieving your dreams and goals?

3. When you find yourself thinking in a habitual and unhelpful way, notice and name the thought pattern. When Lucinda told

herself, 'There's my "I'm not confident" pattern,' she found it easier to challenge herself by behaving in a slightly different way.

4. Read Chapter 26, *Face your fears* (see page 229), to find new ways to challenge yourself.

# SEVEN

# Your best possible self

*'Ten thousand flowers in spring, the moon in autumn, a cool breeze in summer, snow in winter. If your mind isn't clouded by unnecessary things, this is the best season of your life.'*
Wu Men Hui-k'ai, Sung-dynasty Chinese Ch'an monk

Most of us are good at remembering the things that haven't gone well in our lives or recalling our weaknesses, but we often forget about (or downplay) our redeeming qualities and our most meaningful achievements.

In order to create lasting change in our lives, we need to begin by reviewing our relationship with ourselves. If our habit is to be constantly self-critical, it might be hard to even imagine an inspired, confident version of yourself.

Reflecting on the positive aspects of your life will help you create a deeper connection with your most authentic self as well as inviting you to think about who the *best possible you* might be. One of the keys to discovering this version of yourself is maintaining an inward focus and staying true to your own values, rather than getting caught up in ideas of what others want for you or what society deems important.

Take some time now to reflect on the moments in your life when you have felt most alive and the times when you feel that you've been at your best.

## What activities did you love most as a child or teenager?

. . . . . . . . . . . . . . . . . . . . . . . . . . . . . . . . . . . . . . . . . . . . . . .
. . . . . . . . . . . . . . . . . . . . . . . . . . . . . . . . . . . . . . . . . . . . . . .
. . . . . . . . . . . . . . . . . . . . . . . . . . . . . . . . . . . . . . . . . . . . . . .
. . . . . . . . . . . . . . . . . . . . . . . . . . . . . . . . . . . . . . . . . . . . . . .
. . . . . . . . . . . . . . . . . . . . . . . . . . . . . . . . . . . . . . . . . . . . . . .

## What are you proud of?

Make a note of at least ten things you have done in your life that you feel proud of. If you find it difficult to identify significant achievements, include even the small things that feel meaningful to you such as, *Being there for a friend at a time in need* or *Enrolling in Spanish classes.*

. . . . . . . . . . . . . . . . . . . . . . . . . . . . . . . . . . . . . . . . . . . . . . .
. . . . . . . . . . . . . . . . . . . . . . . . . . . . . . . . . . . . . . . . . . . . . . .
. . . . . . . . . . . . . . . . . . . . . . . . . . . . . . . . . . . . . . . . . . . . . . .
. . . . . . . . . . . . . . . . . . . . . . . . . . . . . . . . . . . . . . . . . . . . . . .
. . . . . . . . . . . . . . . . . . . . . . . . . . . . . . . . . . . . . . . . . . . . . . .
. . . . . . . . . . . . . . . . . . . . . . . . . . . . . . . . . . . . . . . . . . . . . . .
. . . . . . . . . . . . . . . . . . . . . . . . . . . . . . . . . . . . . . . . . . . . . . .
. . . . . . . . . . . . . . . . . . . . . . . . . . . . . . . . . . . . . . . . . . . . . . .
. . . . . . . . . . . . . . . . . . . . . . . . . . . . . . . . . . . . . . . . . . . . . . .
. . . . . . . . . . . . . . . . . . . . . . . . . . . . . . . . . . . . . . . . . . . . . . .

**What strengths were you using in the moments you feel proud of?**

. . . . . . . . . . . . . . . . . . . . . . . . . . . . . . . . . . . . .
. . . . . . . . . . . . . . . . . . . . . . . . . . . . . . . . . . . . .
. . . . . . . . . . . . . . . . . . . . . . . . . . . . . . . . . . . . .
. . . . . . . . . . . . . . . . . . . . . . . . . . . . . . . . . . . . .
. . . . . . . . . . . . . . . . . . . . . . . . . . . . . . . . . . . . .
. . . . . . . . . . . . . . . . . . . . . . . . . . . . . . . . . . . . .

**Which activities energise you most?**

What are the activities or interests that restore or 'fill' you when you're feeling depleted?

. . . . . . . . . . . . . . . . . . . . . . . . . . . . . . . . . . . . .
. . . . . . . . . . . . . . . . . . . . . . . . . . . . . . . . . . . . .
. . . . . . . . . . . . . . . . . . . . . . . . . . . . . . . . . . . . .
. . . . . . . . . . . . . . . . . . . . . . . . . . . . . . . . . . . . .
. . . . . . . . . . . . . . . . . . . . . . . . . . . . . . . . . . . . .
. . . . . . . . . . . . . . . . . . . . . . . . . . . . . . . . . . . . .

**In which environments are you at your best?**

Most of us can identify a place or a number of places that energise us or help us to be at our best. We can usually identify the opposite too – the places that deplete us or drain our energy. Make a note of the environmental factors that help you to perform at your best.

. . . . . . . . . . . . . . . . . . . . . . . . . . . . . . . . . . . . .
. . . . . . . . . . . . . . . . . . . . . . . . . . . . . . . . . . . . .
. . . . . . . . . . . . . . . . . . . . . . . . . . . . . . . . . . . . .
. . . . . . . . . . . . . . . . . . . . . . . . . . . . . . . . . . . . .
. . . . . . . . . . . . . . . . . . . . . . . . . . . . . . . . . . . . .
. . . . . . . . . . . . . . . . . . . . . . . . . . . . . . . . . . . . .

**Who brings out the best in you?**

Think about the people who have made you feel understood, seen and validated for being yourself. Another way to think of this is to identify people who can see your 'goodness'.

. . . . . . . . . . . . . . . . . . . . . . . . . . . . . . . . . . . . . . . . . .

. . . . . . . . . . . . . . . . . . . . . . . . . . . . . . . . . . . . . . . . . .

. . . . . . . . . . . . . . . . . . . . . . . . . . . . . . . . . . . . . . . . . .

. . . . . . . . . . . . . . . . . . . . . . . . . . . . . . . . . . . . . . . . . .

. . . . . . . . . . . . . . . . . . . . . . . . . . . . . . . . . . . . . . . . . .

**Remember your peak experiences**

Reflect back to the *peak experiences* exercise on page 24 and recall one or two of your most positive peak memories. Where were you? What were you doing? Who were you with? What skills or strengths were you using?

. . . . . . . . . . . . . . . . . . . . . . . . . . . . . . . . . . . . . . . . . .

. . . . . . . . . . . . . . . . . . . . . . . . . . . . . . . . . . . . . . . . . .

. . . . . . . . . . . . . . . . . . . . . . . . . . . . . . . . . . . . . . . . . .

. . . . . . . . . . . . . . . . . . . . . . . . . . . . . . . . . . . . . . . . . .

**Who are your role models and for which qualities?**

Rather than trying to find a single person who espouses all the qualities you admire, make a note of at least five people you respect and identify the specific characteristics they have that you would like to emulate.

. . . . . . . . . . . . . . . . . . . . . . . . . . . . . . . . . . . . . . . . . .

. . . . . . . . . . . . . . . . . . . . . . . . . . . . . . . . . . . . . . . . . .

. . . . . . . . . . . . . . . . . . . . . . . . . . . . . . . . . . . . . . . . . .

. . . . . . . . . . . . . . . . . . . . . . . . . . . . . . . . . . . . . . . . . .

. . . . . . . . . . . . . . . . . . . . . . . . . . . . . . . . . . . . . . . . . .

**What do you secretly long for?**

There's a depth to the word 'longing' that invites you to look beyond the surface and reflect on your deepest, most heartfelt needs. This question is one you might like to meditate on.

. . . . . . . . . . . . . . . . . . . . . . . . . . . . . . . . . . . . . . . . . . . .

. . . . . . . . . . . . . . . . . . . . . . . . . . . . . . . . . . . . . . . . . . . .

. . . . . . . . . . . . . . . . . . . . . . . . . . . . . . . . . . . . . . . . . . . .

. . . . . . . . . . . . . . . . . . . . . . . . . . . . . . . . . . . . . . . . . . . .

# How do you want to feel?

My client Tony shared with me his vision to own five luxury cars. In my almost 20 years of coaching, he was the first to express such a goal, so I was genuinely curious to understand what this might mean to him once he achieved it.

'Oh, I don't know. They're just something I've always wanted,' he told me.

I asked him to tell me more about the cars. What makes and models did he love? Were the cars he wanted current or vintage models? What colours did he envisage? When and where would he drive (or store) those cars? What did he dream of doing with them, once he had his collection?

Interestingly, as we began to unpack his desire, he realised there was actually only one car he cared about: a vintage Jaguar that was the replica of a car his father had owned. The other cars had been on his list since his teenage years and the longer he reflected, the more he came to recognise that they were merely a symbol of status for him.

We then started to explore what achieving this status might mean. His initial response was 'respect from my peers' but as we delved into this a little more, Tony arrived at the fact that he wanted to feel respected and admired by his wife.

Beneath many of our material desires lies a deeper, more fundamental need. When we are able to connect with the feelings we're trying to achieve, we sometimes discover entirely different goals or new ways to think about a goal that we've held for some time.

Reflect back on the things that you secretly long for and think about *how you'd like to feel* when these desires come true.

. . . . . . . . . . . . . . . . . . . . . . . . . . . . . . . . . . . . . . . . . . . . . . . . . .

. . . . . . . . . . . . . . . . . . . . . . . . . . . . . . . . . . . . . . . . . . . . . . . . . .

. . . . . . . . . . . . . . . . . . . . . . . . . . . . . . . . . . . . . . . . . . . . . . . . . .

. . . . . . . . . . . . . . . . . . . . . . . . . . . . . . . . . . . . . . . . . . . . . . . . . .

. . . . . . . . . . . . . . . . . . . . . . . . . . . . . . . . . . . . . . . . . . . . . . . . . .

# Your authentic self

Each of us is born with a core version of ourselves. This is the version of you that includes the characteristics, the preferences and the desires that give you an overall sense of your true identity.

From as early as when we were babies, we start losing touch with this core self and instead adapt to become the version of ourselves that develops in response to external pressures. We shape ourselves to fit other people's expectations in an effort to do the right thing by other people (very often our parents) and in order to be accepted in the world.

In finding your way to your true desires, the first step is to reconnect with your true self.

When you're not being true to yourself, you'll find yourself operating at a suboptimal level in many areas of your life. On the flip side, when you feel connected with your true self, everything seems to flow.

~

Consider your *true self* the precursor to your *best possible self*. The latter will be the version of you that is the most energised, inspired and creative. It's where you'll make a genuine connection with your most heartfelt desires, rather than focusing on other people's ideas and opinions about what constitutes a good life. When we lose touch with our *hearts* and try to *think* our way to a meaningful life, we're more likely to compare ourselves with others and pursue goals and dreams that are measured against standards that don't really matter to us. When you tune in to your heart, you'll discover the pathway to the things that make you genuinely happy.

~

Take some time now to reflect on your life story, your needs, your values, your strengths, your habitual patterns of thinking and your responses to the questions at the start of this chapter, and consider how you would describe the most authentic and inspired version of yourself.

You might find it easiest to do this by imagining you're able to observe the truest version of yourself, as though through the eyes of an outsider. See if you can separate from your ego — the part of you that judges yourself as good/bad or successful/unsuccessful — and instead, view your preferences from a factual and unbiased perspective. As you reflect on your values, strengths and even weaknesses, start to recognise that there's nothing at all wrong with any of the choices you make – you simply have a set of preferences for who you are, what you value and the person you'd like to be in this world.

Imagine that you can put aside any concerns about what others think, about who might approve or disapprove and who you might be letting down if you were being the truest version of yourself.

Choose a time in the future (maybe five or ten years from now) and imagine you have become your *best possible self.* What kind of person would you be, what new relationships would you have, which interests would you have embraced, and how do you think you'd feel?

. . . . . . . . . . . . . . . . . . . . . . . . . . . . . . . . . . . . . . . . . . .

. . . . . . . . . . . . . . . . . . . . . . . . . . . . . . . . . . . . . . . . . . .

. . . . . . . . . . . . . . . . . . . . . . . . . . . . . . . . . . . . . . . . . . .

. . . . . . . . . . . . . . . . . . . . . . . . . . . . . . . . . . . . . . . . . . .

. . . . . . . . . . . . . . . . . . . . . . . . . . . . . . . . . . . . . . . . . . .

Describe this version of yourself in present tense language, imagining that you embody all of the qualities you value. For example,

*'I am calm and confident and known for being considerate and thoughtful in all of my relationships. I am patient with my partner and tolerant when they are forgetful. I recognise that we're both a long way from perfect and I forgive us both for our flaws. I have a small handful of truly wonderful friends and I make*

*time to socialise with them a couple of times each week. I listen
to my children mindfully and refrain from offering too much
advice. I respect that they want to find their own way in life.
I take great care of my body and mind – eating well most days,
exercising every morning and giving myself permission to rest or
do something I love for at least a few hours every week.'*

. . . . . . . . . . . . . . . . . . . . . . . . . . . . . . . . . . . . . . . . . .
. . . . . . . . . . . . . . . . . . . . . . . . . . . . . . . . . . . . . . . . . .
. . . . . . . . . . . . . . . . . . . . . . . . . . . . . . . . . . . . . . . . . .
. . . . . . . . . . . . . . . . . . . . . . . . . . . . . . . . . . . . . . . . . .
. . . . . . . . . . . . . . . . . . . . . . . . . . . . . . . . . . . . . . . . . .
. . . . . . . . . . . . . . . . . . . . . . . . . . . . . . . . . . . . . . . . . .
. . . . . . . . . . . . . . . . . . . . . . . . . . . . . . . . . . . . . . . . . .
. . . . . . . . . . . . . . . . . . . . . . . . . . . . . . . . . . . . . . . . . .
. . . . . . . . . . . . . . . . . . . . . . . . . . . . . . . . . . . . . . . . . .
. . . . . . . . . . . . . . . . . . . . . . . . . . . . . . . . . . . . . . . . . .
. . . . . . . . . . . . . . . . . . . . . . . . . . . . . . . . . . . . . . . . . .
. . . . . . . . . . . . . . . . . . . . . . . . . . . . . . . . . . . . . . . . . .
. . . . . . . . . . . . . . . . . . . . . . . . . . . . . . . . . . . . . . . . . .
. . . . . . . . . . . . . . . . . . . . . . . . . . . . . . . . . . . . . . . . . .
. . . . . . . . . . . . . . . . . . . . . . . . . . . . . . . . . . . . . . . . . .
. . . . . . . . . . . . . . . . . . . . . . . . . . . . . . . . . . . . . . . . . .
. . . . . . . . . . . . . . . . . . . . . . . . . . . . . . . . . . . . . . . . . .
. . . . . . . . . . . . . . . . . . . . . . . . . . . . . . . . . . . . . . . . . .
. . . . . . . . . . . . . . . . . . . . . . . . . . . . . . . . . . . . . . . . . .

# EIGHT

# A vision for your ideal life

*'Your vision will become clear only when you look into your heart.
Who looks outside, dreams. Who looks inside, awakens.'*

Carl Jung

Imagery is the most fundamental language we have. Everything we do is processed through images. When we recall events from our past or childhood, we often remember images and emotions. Images aren't necessarily limited to the visual; they can be sounds, tastes, smells or a combination of sensations.

To understand how simple visualisation can invoke a powerful response from your senses, think, for example, of holding a fresh, juicy lemon in your hand. Imagine you can feel the texture and see the vividness of its yellow skin. Picture slicing the lemon in half and watching the juice drip – imagine you can smell the strong citrus scent. Now visualise putting the lemon in your mouth, sucking on it and tasting the sour, acidic flavour of the juice.

If you are like most people, your salivary glands will react as though you have really tasted a lemon and your mouth will water a little.

Unfortunately, we don't always use visualisation in a positive way. Much of the daydreaming we habitually do is in the form of worry. As you now know, our minds are attracted to negative thoughts more than positive ones. In primitive times, this served us well. In order to stay alive, we needed to approach the world with caution. These days, we're still on the alert for things that might pose a risk, which makes our minds overly vigilant, and this negative thinking can become a problem.

Positive visualisation is a practice that can help us to identify possibilities and move towards our dreams. When you give yourself time to relax and explore your version of an ideal life, you begin to create a mental image of what it is you're hoping to achieve. Visualisation not only helps to ground you, making it possible to believe in your dreams, it also helps you respond proactively to the opportunities that life presents.

When I first learned about this process, I was sceptical about it. There wasn't a body of science behind it and what research I could find focused mostly on creating material wealth, which wasn't really resonating with me.

Then I heard clients share how they were using this process to create meaningful change in their lives.

So one January morning, a decade ago now, I allowed myself to approach this exercise with a sense of lightness. I sat down at my desk, reflected on my values and wrote a few sentences that later became my ten-year vision. I thought about how this vision could help me live a more purposeful, meaningful and generous life.

I imagined every aspect of my ideal life. I included the work I would do, the interests I'd have, how I would nurture my relationships, how I'd take care of my health and how I would make a greater contribution in other people's lives and give back to the planet.

I shared my vision with Chris and fine-tuned the elements to match his dreams and then crafted a beautiful picture for our shared lives. I even went as far as sketching the floor plan of our next home, with space for our daughters to stay and room for grandchildren (if they arrived one day). I drew a verandah on the north-western side of the house and made a note of where the sea would be. I imagined the gum trees, the veggie garden and the walks we would take in nature each day.

Later, I filled the pinboard behind my desk with images of the house, the garden and the driveway as well as other pictures representing the creativity, connection, contribution and wellbeing I envisaged in our lives. I made a smaller collage of those images on my laptop and printed it out to pin inside my wardrobe. I wrote a list of goals that related to each area of the vision, and chose one small action step to take in the coming weeks to move me towards our dream.

I kept up these creative exercises at the beginning of each new year and while the image of my ideal life was never far from my mind, I often wondered if it was anything more than an indulgent form of dreaming.

Then, three years ago, when I was right on the cusp of giving up on our dream, a series of serendipitous events changed my thinking.

Chris and I had been in the Northern Beaches region in Sydney, shooting a series of videos for a client's new business. As we walked along the beach after breakfast each morning, we realised that surrounded by towering gum trees, native birdlife and the ocean, we were momentarily immersed in our vision. As we flew home, I chose to see our time in Sydney as a sign that the world was telling me, 'It's time.' Two weeks later, we put our home of 25 years on the market.

While we settled on a different location and a different kind of property from the one we had originally dreamed of, we stayed connected with the most fundamental elements of our vision. We focused on *how we wanted to live* and *how we wanted to feel* in our new lives.

At the top of the list was simplicity. We wanted to slow down and make a stronger connection with nature. To grow our own food, to spend more time outside, to cultivate a thriving vegetable garden and to hopefully one day become self-sufficient. To have a space that our children and grandchildren would call an oasis, a place where we could work and be creative. We wanted a peaceful life, where we could cook for friends, plant a few trees, run meditation classes from home and share our abundance with others.

After a few months searching for our new home, we found ourselves inspecting a house that was almost an exact match for my seven-year-old floor plan sketch. It sat on the hillside on a small acreage, with a deck along the north-western side and the sea just beyond. The gum tree–lined driveway was a replica of the image that had been on my pinboard for years. While the location was ten minutes down the road from our ideal spot and there was no view of the water (unless you stood on the roof or counted the dam), I realised that in every other way, this was our dream home.

~

Shakti Gawain was well ahead of her time when she wrote her best-selling book, *Creative Visualization*, in 1978. She believed creative visualisation to be the powerful process of using your imagination to create emotional, spiritual or physical change in your life. In her book, Shakti suggests that without even realising it, all of us use imagery every day to create our reality, but because of deep-seated and unconscious negative patterns of thinking, the lives we create are often limited.

She shares a range of techniques that centre around the practices of relaxing into a meditative state of mind and creating a detailed image of something new or different in our lives.

Shakti's belief is that energy is magnetic – our thoughts and feelings create a form of energy that attracts similar energy. She believes that there are unseen forces at play in the universe and when we can tap into those forces, we create positive change in our lives.

Before beginning the process of visualisation, Shakti suggests we acknowledge the law of energy and start to notice how our thoughts and feelings are attracting energy of a similar nature. What we create in our lives, she says, is first created in thought form. Whatever we think about most, whatever we imagine most vividly, is what we begin to manifest.

Shakti writes, 'The process of change does not occur on superficial levels, through mere "positive thinking." It involves exploring, discovering, and changing our deepest, most basic *attitudes towards life*.'

# The creative visualisation process

Before you draft your vision for your ideal life, you might like to try the creative visualisation process for a smaller change you'd like to see.

For example, imagine hearing from a certain friend or seeing a specific object in the coming days. Don't be discouraged if it doesn't work immediately – it takes time to alter your usual patterns of thinking. In an ideal world, engage in this practice every day, but it's also helpful to note that Shakti's belief is that it still works if you focus less frequently.

## Meditate or relax

Get into a deep state of relaxation by either meditating or listening to a guided body scan meditation.

## Visualise

Once you feel deeply relaxed, bring to mind something you would like to have or do or work towards in your life. This can be any kind of change – a new friend or partner, a new job or home, or maybe a change within yourself or your family. Imagine in as much detail as possible, and once you have the mental picture, think of it as already existing. Imagine yourself immersed in this new situation, as if it were real. If you find it hard to create mental imagery, just *think about* the change you're seeking. When you're first starting out, choose smaller goals that are easier to believe in. Later you can work up to more significant or more challenging goals.

## Feel a sense of appreciation

With the image in your mind, make a positive statement or affirmation about the change and feel a sense of appreciation for it, for example, 'I welcome a peaceful new home' or 'I am ready for a new role working with great colleagues' or 'I am becoming more confident'. My personal preference is to make sure your affirmations feel believable, so rather than saying, 'I am now in a loving relationship' if you're not, use an affirmation such as, 'I welcome a loving partner into my life'. After focusing on your affirmation, say 'thank you' for this new experience, as if it were already real. If you notice doubts arising, just do your best to allow them to flow through you.

## Focus often on your vision and how it makes you feel

While you don't want to become overly fixated on the changes you're trying to create, it's helpful to bring your vision to mind often and to imagine how you'll feel once you're immersed in your ideal life. Focus on it in a relaxed and positive way and continue to feel appreciation towards it.

## Keep the energy flowing in your life

Tap into the universal law of abundance by allowing energy to flow in your life. Give love and kindness, give away possessions you no longer need and spend or donate a little more freely. Equally, be willing to accept kindness or offers of support from others. The idea is to keep all forms of energy flowing in and out in your life.

## Don't try too hard

Creative visualisation is not about exerting effort or trying to force your goals to happen. Rather, it's about cultivating a positive state of mind and trusting that you are moving towards your version of an ideal life. It's highly possible (as it was in my life) that some aspects of your vision won't be exactly as you'd imagined – which is fine. Stay focused on how you want to feel and the values you most want to align yourself with.

### Take small action steps

Choose a few small action steps that move you in the direction of your dreams. Research new roles, join a dating app, visit the location you're planning to move to – create a degree of forward momentum as a way of signalling to the universe that you're genuinely ready for change.

## Create your own vision

Set aside an hour or two to write out your vision statement for five or ten years from now. If you want to create significant change, a longer time frame gives you the freedom to envision a life that is very different from now. It's also useful to note that a meaningful life may well include many aspects from your current existence with just a few minor adjustments.

Connect with your intuition and trust that you know what you want in your vision. Write by hand to slow you down and to allow your imagination time to create a detailed picture of your ideal life. Be as descriptive as possible about all aspects and write your vision in the present tense – as though you're already fully immersed in your new world. Imagine how you'll feel once your vision is achieved, while keeping in mind the most important values you wish to espouse.

If you find it difficult to get started, begin with, *It's a Saturday afternoon and I'm at home with* . . . Describe the people closest to you, where you are living, the kind of work you do and any creative or other interests you're engaged in. Add as much detail as you can about the person you are in this vision.

Do your best to put aside all your usual limiting thoughts as you dream about the life you would create *if anything was possible*. Keep your focus broad enough to include details about each of the following areas:

- Who are the most important people in your life?
- What kind of relationships do you have with them?
- What kind of person are you?
- Where do you live?
- What kind of home do you live in?
- How do you spend your days?
- What work are you doing?
- How are you contributing to your community and the planet?
- What are your interests?
- How do you take care of your health and wellbeing?
- What's your financial situation?
- How do you express yourself creatively?
- How do you connect spiritually?
- What are you learning about?
- What impact are you having on the world?

# Create a visual representation of your vision

Once you have completed the written version of your vision, create a visual representation of your ideal life in any format that feels appealing to you. Some people sketch or paint their vision; others prefer to gather a bunch of magazines and cut out images that they add to a pinboard.

My personal preference is to create two versions – a pinboard of images as well as an online version using software on my laptop or an application such as Canva (a graphic design program that uses 'drag and drop' methodology making it easy for non-designers to use). I gather images from my own photo collection (these are usually of people and places I love) and I jump onto stock image websites to find photos that fill the gaps. This is a pretty time-consuming process but it's also a lot of fun.

Once you've created your visual record, print or photocopy your document so you have a few copies. Put them where you can see them every day. Even if you're not actively engaged with your vision every day, research suggests that the subliminal message it creates will help you to move in the direction of your dreams.

## If you're still stuck

If you're still not ready to write out your vision, put it aside for now and instead, write a list of 100 things you would like to achieve or do or be in your lifetime.

Before you complete this activity, engage in a pastime that helps you to physically relax. Exercise, meditate, take a yoga class or go for a long walk in nature. Do whatever you can to help you to connect with your intuition so you can feel your way to the answers that are best for you.

When you're ready to make a start on your list, as well as adding what you want to achieve, include how you want to feel, who you want to connect with, what you want to learn and how you want to be in the world.

Once your '100 things' list is complete, scan back across it and see if you have any insights into the elements that matter most in your life. Are there any recurring themes that point you in a certain direction? Can your list help you to see what is currently missing from your life?

When you do identify themes, consider how they fit with your values. For example, a range of entries about travel might tie in with your value of adventure or numerous points about time spent with friends may give you clarity about the changes you'd like to make in your social life.

# Look for synchronicity

In the months leading up to us finding our new home, we experienced several serendipitous events. They were the first in a series that I later identified as 'synchronicity' – the term Swiss psychologist Carl Jung coined as a way of describing how sometimes seemingly unrelated events can appear meaningful if we choose to look at them more closely.

Unlike some traditional cultures which held the belief that unexplained related events were the work of spiritual forces, Jung believed that such coincidences might be the work of the 'collective unconscious'. He believed they might be another way of adding meaning to our lives and better understanding the relationship between ourselves and the wider world.

When we tune in to moments of synchronicity, they can offer messages in our lives. Jung suggested that instead of asking what caused the coincidence, we should ask, *What's the message that accompanies it?*

## How to notice synchronicity in your life

Meditate more often, and during your meditation, or at the end of it, feel a connection with something bigger than yourself. This might be as simple as imagining an expansion in the boundaries of your body and an awareness that at a cellular level, we have a connection to all living beings and the natural world.

During your day, bring your awareness into the present moment. Pay attention to your surroundings and the experience of being connected with what's around you.

Pay attention to coincidences in your life and be curious about the messages they might be signalling.

# NINE

# What gives your life meaning?

*'You cannot get through a single day without having an impact on the world around you. What you do makes a difference, and you have to decide what kind of difference you want to make.'*

Jane Goodall

In the September of 1942, Austrian psychiatrist and neurologist Dr Viktor Frankl was arrested in Vienna with his wife, parents and other family members and later, deported to a Nazi concentration camp.

Working as a psychiatrist to the inmates in the camps, Dr Frankl came to believe that the only way to survive his ordeal was to hold on to a sense of meaning. For him, that meaning came from helping his fellow prisoners and also from his deep and abiding love for his wife Tilly.

Not knowing if his wife was alive while he was in the camp, his love for her was his motivation to keep going. He reflected that the only thing that could not be taken from a person is their own attitude towards a situation.

In 1945, when Frankl was freed and he learned of his wife's passing, he returned home to Vienna to carry on his work. He observed that one of the reasons other people managed to survive the camps was that they too had focused on finding meaning.

Frankl's belief was that meaning is best discovered as the by-product of pursuing other goals rather than a single pursuit in itself. We find it most readily when we embrace activities that connect us with something bigger than ourselves, for example when we pursue knowledge, do purposeful work, care for others, express love, find courage in the face of adversity and overcome suffering.

As well as seeking a *greater* sense of meaning, Frankl believed we must look at how we can make *each individual moment* valuable and meaningful. He recognised that it was possible, even in the most painful circumstances, for a person to find meaning and hope, for example in the beauty of art and nature. Frankl noted that his fellow prisoners marvelled at the views of mountains glimpsed through the windows of their train on their voyage to a Bavarian camp, despite knowing where they were headed.

When we seek beauty, love or justice, we find that a meaningful life is as much about appreciating the beauty in the given moment as it is about pursuing experiences that fascinate us, doing the right thing and loving fully. We do these things not just because we are seeking meaning in life but because they are valuable and good in themselves.

~

Andre's life was at a pinnacle. He had just achieved a promotion in his law firm, he'd finished renovating his 1960s apartment and his boyfriend of 12 months was about to move in.

Now that he'd reached a point where he had his life largely in order, Andre was looking for a way to make peace with some of his lingering emotional pain. Growing up in a conservative family and attending a religious school, coming to terms with his sexual identity had been a difficult experience for Andre. His teenage years were a period of confusion and loneliness and at times, he felt deeply depressed.

Andre's sense was that his own healing might come about through helping others who found themselves in the position he'd been in just two decades earlier.

He found a role mentoring young men who were trying to work out their sexual preferences. Remembering how isolating it had been with no one to talk to, Andre wanted to ensure other young people were not on their own as they navigated the complex path of learning about who they were. As he suspected, giving back in this way went a long way to healing his own pain and he later recognised that mentoring others was a calling he could also pursue in his work.

## What gives your life meaning?

Think about the experiences that help you transcend the everyday-ness of your life. These are the moments that may feel as though they connect you to something bigger than yourself. They might be as simple as seeing a beautiful sunset, feeling connected to someone you love, savouring a meal or spending time in nature.

. . . . . . . . . . . . . . . . . . . . . . . . . . . . . . . . . . . . . . . . . . .
. . . . . . . . . . . . . . . . . . . . . . . . . . . . . . . . . . . . . . . . . . .
. . . . . . . . . . . . . . . . . . . . . . . . . . . . . . . . . . . . . . . . . . .
. . . . . . . . . . . . . . . . . . . . . . . . . . . . . . . . . . . . . . . . . . .
. . . . . . . . . . . . . . . . . . . . . . . . . . . . . . . . . . . . . . . . . . .

# Discover your life purpose

People often get stuck when they begin searching for their life purpose because they feel that it needs to be lofty or life-changing. Discovering your purpose is about exploring *why you do what you do* and thinking about what it is that gives meaning to your work, your relationships and your life.

While it's tempting to look for a life purpose that will change the world in some way, it's generally easier to begin with a focus that is fulfilling and meaningful at a personal level.

Read through the following questions and answer each as honestly as you can. Think about the things that come naturally to you, put aside your humility and acknowledge all of your natural gifts. Don't dismiss anything as unimportant or not significant enough.

- How do I already make a difference in other people's lives?
- What are the most significant challenges I have overcome in my life?
- What are the most important lessons I have learned?
- What are the injustices that touch me most deeply?

- What pain have I experienced and overcome that drives me to want to help others?
- What is the work that most energises me?
- What are the things I feel instinctively 'called' to do?
- In what ways could I share my calling with others?
- What am I willing to make sacrifices for?
- When I put aside humility, what are my unique gifts?
- What are the causes I'm most passionate about?
- What impact would I like to have in the world?
- What is one thing I'd love to be remembered for most?
- What do I have to give?

# Examples of other people's life purpose

- To help people discover their uniqueness and believe in themselves.
- To advocate for those who have less of a voice than I do.
- To be a loving and nurturing parent and partner and to create a home that makes my family feel safe and secure.
- To help people recognise their own goodness so that they might go out into the world with confidence and do the things they truly love.
- To help others see the humour and lightness in life.
- To help people believe in themselves.
- To help people grow and develop by sharing my wisdom and fostering a love of learning.
- To create beautiful art that inspires others to learn about themselves or create objects of beauty of their own.
- To live a spiritual life and to share my teachings with others.

## Look for the themes

Review your responses from the exercises in previous chapters and identify any themes that run through your answers. Look at your story, your values, your strengths and your best possible self exercises and identify any themes or any insights. For example, as I reflected on my own life, I recognised that from a very young age, time spent in nature, immersed in books, as well as my experience of always being the new girl at school, were recurring themes from my childhood. My books were my constant friends and reading was where I learned about people and what made them tick. Hours spent alone in the natural world was where I found myself most at peace. Later, in my adult life, I came to see that these solo pursuits were largely the result of my family's constant moving around and my lack of consistent friendships. While I didn't often feel lonely as a child, the experience of being an outsider gave me access to solitary pursuits that remain an important part of my adult life, as well as a greater sense of empathy for people who sit on the fringes.

. . . . . . . . . . . . . . . . . . . . . . . . . . . . . . . . . . . . . . . .
. . . . . . . . . . . . . . . . . . . . . . . . . . . . . . . . . . . . . . . .
. . . . . . . . . . . . . . . . . . . . . . . . . . . . . . . . . . . . . . . .
. . . . . . . . . . . . . . . . . . . . . . . . . . . . . . . . . . . . . . . .
. . . . . . . . . . . . . . . . . . . . . . . . . . . . . . . . . . . . . . . .
. . . . . . . . . . . . . . . . . . . . . . . . . . . . . . . . . . . . . . . .
. . . . . . . . . . . . . . . . . . . . . . . . . . . . . . . . . . . . . . . .
. . . . . . . . . . . . . . . . . . . . . . . . . . . . . . . . . . . . . . . .
. . . . . . . . . . . . . . . . . . . . . . . . . . . . . . . . . . . . . . . .

# My purpose is . . .

Reflecting on your insights above, now think about *how you'd like to contribute* and *who you'd like to contribute to*. Consider the challenges you've overcome in your own life and how you might share that wisdom with others. Think about the world issues that concern you most as well as the obstacles that friends or family members have encountered or overcome that have touched you.

Take out your journal or use the space on page 78 and write at the top of the page, *My purpose is . . .* and complete the sentence by writing anything that comes into your mind. If you find it hard to get started, use an example from pages 75–6.

As you do this exercise, don't try to force your answers. Just begin by putting pen to paper and writing from a stream of consciousness. You may find that you need to fill a few pages.

Keep writing until you feel a sense of emotional connection with your answers and you discover an answer that feels pretty right. (A side note here is that it doesn't need to feel perfect – just get it to a point where you know you're close.) Take as long as you need. This might be an exercise to come back to a few days after your first attempt.

My purpose is . . . . . . . . . . . . . . . . . . . . . . . . . . . . . . . . . . . . . . . . . . . . .
. . . . . . . . . . . . . . . . . . . . . . . . . . . . . . . . . . . . . . . . . . . . . . . . . . . . . . . .
. . . . . . . . . . . . . . . . . . . . . . . . . . . . . . . . . . . . . . . . . . . . . . . . . . . . . . . .
. . . . . . . . . . . . . . . . . . . . . . . . . . . . . . . . . . . . . . . . . . . . . . . . . . . . . . . .
. . . . . . . . . . . . . . . . . . . . . . . . . . . . . . . . . . . . . . . . . . . . . . . . . . . . . . . .
. . . . . . . . . . . . . . . . . . . . . . . . . . . . . . . . . . . . . . . . . . . . . . . . . . . . . . . .
. . . . . . . . . . . . . . . . . . . . . . . . . . . . . . . . . . . . . . . . . . . . . . . . . . . . . . . .

# How will you know if you have discovered your life purpose?

- You feel a strong emotional connection with it.
- The thought of pursuing it energises you.
- You feel inspired and creative.
- It gives your life (and your work) meaning.
- You feel more patient about achieving your goals and dreams because you know you are on the right path.
- Pursuing your purpose might mean increasing your workload but instead of feeling drained, the idea of this fills you with energy and enthusiasm.

# TEN

# Side-step your excuses

*'Life is a series of natural and spontaneous changes. Don't resist them; that only creates sorrow. Let reality be reality. Let things flow naturally forward in whatever way they like.'*

Lao Tzu

In the same way that I almost gave up on my long-held dream, you might be telling yourself to appreciate what you have right now or to be grateful for the things that are already good in your life. Sometimes completing the vision exercise *does* help us to recognise that we have everything we need in our lives, but equally, try to catch yourself if you're making excuses about why you couldn't do or have the things you actually aspire to.

Maybe, like some of my clients, you're not allowing yourself to dream of a different life because you're immersed in the belief that *people like you* aren't worthy of such things. You might be fearful to put something on paper because you worry that you won't get it right or you'd never be able to achieve such lofty dreams. Maybe you're worried you'll change your mind or make things worse than they are right now. All these thoughts and fears are a normal part of the process.

When you're unclear about what to include in your vision, try thinking about it when you're away from your everyday environments and routines. While you're in a new place, you can often see things through new eyes and you may find, as I did, that you realise you've known what you wanted all along.

If after trying that, your vision is still unclear, make something up, even if it doesn't feel entirely accurate. Then walk away from it for a week or two. When you revisit this version of your dream, you might be surprised at how easy it is to modify the aspects that don't feel right. Over time your subconscious mind will do some of the work for you and your vision may seem to miraculously come to life.

When you do finally have clarity about the vision you want to pursue, it's also natural to experience fear or apprehension as you work towards your goals. What if you can't achieve them? What if you don't love your new life or what if something goes wrong along the way?

Change and uncertainty are the only inevitable factors in all our lives. Each of us will encounter adversity, regardless of whether we pursue our dreams or not. Instead of not starting, remind yourself that the greatest sense of regret usually occurs when we don't even give ourselves a chance at all. If the goal you're working towards doesn't eventuate or if you find yourself faced with some unexpected hardship in the pursuit of it, you'll find a way to carry on. You'll learn about yourself and you'll discover new strengths as well as your capacity for resilience.

This was certainly the case for me. Soon after we moved into our new home, our lives took a much less fortunate turn. Just three weeks after arriving, Chris had a diagnosis of cancer. I remember sitting across the breakfast table, looking at this strong and healthy husband of mine who had never had a sick day in the 30 years we'd been together. How could he possibly be so unwell?

I wondered how he would survive this health challenge and how we'd manage our new acreage and pay our mortgage at the same time. Together we reflected on the irony of the timing and then realised that had we not made the move when we did, we would never have made it at all.

Here we were, immersed in this beautiful, peaceful setting with the kookaburras welcoming each new day, with a family of wood ducks on the dam, rosellas and galahs in the gum trees and the winter sun arcing around into the living room. There was something about being in this healing environment that felt inherently right. The situation we found ourselves in was far from perfect, but we braced ourselves to tackle one of the more difficult challenges of our lives.

As you'll read in Chapter 21, *Create possibility* (page 194), we all make assumptions about ourselves that limit what we set out to achieve. We have ideas about what a good person should or shouldn't do and we are overly influenced by other people's opinions.

You might believe you're not confident enough, not attractive enough, not smart enough, not outgoing enough or too old. Maybe you tell yourself you need to wait until you fit into your favourite dress, have a bit more time on your hands or land a better job before you start pursuing a happier life.

My client Vanessa had many reasons not to start dating. Her work was too busy, she wasn't a fan of dating apps and she believed the 'right' way to meet someone was to connect naturally. As we spoke, our conversation turned to her fear that not finding a partner would impact her long-time dream of becoming a mother.

Having been single for six years, Vanessa realised that while her goal of becoming a parent was partly outside her control, she was also creating significant barriers. Her partnerless status had become intertwined with a sense of shame and fear and a creeping sense of desperation as she approached 38. Not wanting to appear vulnerable, Vanessa wasn't comfortable to talk to her friends so she carried this burden on her own and felt increasingly isolated. She worried that she'd left it too late.

The first step we took was to get clear about her vision for a life as a mother. In an ideal world, Vanessa wanted to share that experience with a partner rather than having a child on her own. Without making a concerted effort to meet someone over the next few years, Vanessa's chances of achieving her dream would narrow. She agreed that despite her fear, she needed to give herself every opportunity so that even if she did end up having a child on her own, she would have no regrets about not having tried.

Before she undertook what she felt was the daunting task of putting herself into the world of online dating, we worked together to uncover and reframe her excuses.

## Put aside your excuses

Use the following prompts to help you craft a list of the excuses you typically make when it comes to creating change in your life. After completing the exercise, look back over your excuses and think about how these are holding you back in making changes that could make your life more meaningful.

*Because I'm* . . . . . . . . . . . . . . . . . . . . . . . *I can't* . . . . . . . .

. . . . . . . . . . . . . . . . . . . . . . . . . . . . . . . . . . . . . . . . . . . . . . .

*Because* . . . . . . . . . . . . . . . . . . . . . *happened to me,*
*I haven't felt confident to* . . . . . . . . . . . . . . . . . . . . . . . . . . . . .

*If I was more* . . . . . . . . . . . . . . . . . . . . . . . *I would be doing*

. . . . . . . . . . . . . . . . . . . . . . . . . . . . . . . . . . . . . . . . . . . . . . .

*Because my family was* . . . . . . . . . . . . . . . . . . . . . . . . . . . . .
*I couldn't* . . . . . . . . . . . . . . . . . . . . . . . . . . . . . . . . . . . . . . . .

*If only I was* . . . . . . . . . . . . . . . . . . . . . . *I would be ready*
*to* . . . . . . . . . . . . . . . . . . . . . . . . . . . . . . . . . . . . . . . . . . . . .

*Because I'm* . . . . . . . . . . . . . . . . . . . . . . . . . . . . . . . . . . . . . .
*I have never* . . . . . . . . . . . . . . . . . . . . . . . . . . . . . . . . . . . . . .

*I'll be ready to start once I've* . . . . . . . . . . . . . . . . . . . . . . . . . .

*I should* . . . . . . . . . . . . . . . . . . . . . . . . . . . . . . . . . . . . . . . . .

*I shouldn't* . . . . . . . . . . . . . . . . . . . . . . . . . . . . . . . . . . . . . .

# Reframe your excuses

For each of the statements above, create a 'reframe'.

*Because* . . . . . . . . . . . . . . . . . . . . . . . . . . . . . . . . . . . . . . . . .
*happened to me, I now want to.* . . . . . . . . . . . . . . . . . . . . . . . . .

*Now that I am* . . . . . . . . . . . . . . . . . . . . . . . . . . . . . . . . . . . . .
*I am ready to.* . . . . . . . . . . . . . . . . . . . . . . . . . . . . . . . . . . . . . .

*Because I'm* . . . . . . . . . . . . . . . . . . . . . . . . . . . . . . . . . . . . . .
*I will now.* . . . . . . . . . . . . . . . . . . . . . . . . . . . . . . . . . . . . . . . .

*Even though I'm not* . . . . . . . . . . . . . . . . . . . . . . . . . . . . . . . .

*I'm going to* . . . . . . . . . . . . . . . . . . . . . . . . . . . . . . . . . . . . . . . . . . . . . .
    *I give myself permission to* . . . . . . . . . . . . . . . . . . . . . . . . . . . . . . . .

## Reflection

Look back across the previous ten chapters and reflect on what you've learned about yourself. Have you had insights into the person you really are? If you were being your best possible self and you had the courage to pursue your ideal life, what kind of life would that be? What can you do to signal to yourself and the world that you're really open to change? And what excuses do you need to put aside?

Create some positive energy in the coming week by noting below a few small adjustments you can make. Include below at least three things you feel you can solidly commit to that will at least move you in the direction of your dreams and schedule them into your diary.

. . . . . . . . . . . . . . . . . . . . . . . . . . . . . . . . . . . . . . . . . . . . . . . . . . . .
. . . . . . . . . . . . . . . . . . . . . . . . . . . . . . . . . . . . . . . . . . . . . . . . . . . .
. . . . . . . . . . . . . . . . . . . . . . . . . . . . . . . . . . . . . . . . . . . . . . . . . . . .
. . . . . . . . . . . . . . . . . . . . . . . . . . . . . . . . . . . . . . . . . . . . . . . . . . . .
. . . . . . . . . . . . . . . . . . . . . . . . . . . . . . . . . . . . . . . . . . . . . . . . . . . .
. . . . . . . . . . . . . . . . . . . . . . . . . . . . . . . . . . . . . . . . . . . . . . . . . . . .
. . . . . . . . . . . . . . . . . . . . . . . . . . . . . . . . . . . . . . . . . . . . . . . . . . . .
. . . . . . . . . . . . . . . . . . . . . . . . . . . . . . . . . . . . . . . . . . . . . . . . . . . .
. . . . . . . . . . . . . . . . . . . . . . . . . . . . . . . . . . . . . . . . . . . . . . . . . . . .
. . . . . . . . . . . . . . . . . . . . . . . . . . . . . . . . . . . . . . . . . . . . . . . . . . . .
. . . . . . . . . . . . . . . . . . . . . . . . . . . . . . . . . . . . . . . . . . . . . . . . . . . .
. . . . . . . . . . . . . . . . . . . . . . . . . . . . . . . . . . . . . . . . . . . . . . . . . . . .

# PART TWO

# Change your life

# ELEVEN

# Change your thinking

*'In the end, only three things matter: how much you loved,
how gently you lived, and how gracefully you let go of
things not meant for you.'*

Jack Kornfield

We often believe that it's external events that cause our happiness
or unhappiness, but it's equally true that how we think about those
events impacts our life satisfaction too.

Many of our thoughts (and as a result, our feelings and behaviours)
are automatic and not in our conscious awareness. When we tune in
and become more cognisant of our habitual patterns of thinking, we
start to see how those thoughts impact our actions and how, in turn,
our actions can sometimes inhibit our wellbeing.

Over the next 19 chapters, I'll share philosophies and therapies
that can change your thinking and change your life. I have formal
training in some and others are concepts I introduce to clients, as
I'll introduce them to you, in the hope that you can explore them
further with a qualified therapist.

You'll find that there's a fair amount of overlap in the concepts, with each being designed to help you understand how your automatic thoughts and feelings are impacting the way you feel about yourself and how these thoughts and feelings are playing a part in your life choices.

It's my hope that within these chapters and the case studies, you'll see some of yourself. With a greater sense of awareness and, hopefully, a little more self-acceptance, you'll find a way to balance *appreciating the things that are good in your life right now* with *working towards your dreams*.

~

'We think that the point is to pass the test or overcome the problem, but the truth is that things don't really get solved. They come together and they fall apart. Then they come together again and fall apart again. It's just like that. The healing comes from letting there be room for all of this to happen: room for grief, for relief, for misery, for joy.'

Pema Chödrön

~

Regardless of your current circumstances or your history, it's worth remembering that you have a choice in how you interact with your story. You can be characterised in both positive and negative ways by everything that has happened to you but past events don't need to define you.

I've worked with clients who've experienced great trauma as well as some who've had only minor disappointments in their lives. There's no predicting who will hold on to anger, resentment and bitterness and who will move forward with forgiveness and hope. What I have learned is that every day is an opportunity to choose your approach once again and even when you've spent decades telling yourself there's some kind of 'block' holding you back, there is great power in the very practical decision to get on with it, regardless.

Mindful awareness will help you to accept all that you've experienced in your life to date and self-compassion will help you to see that the moments of pain or betrayal don't need to be a reason to shield yourself from a joyous and loving life.

If you have the sense that opening up to your true emotions or revisiting past hurts is going to be too much to deal with on your own, make an appointment with your GP and ask them to recommend a good therapist.

## The happiest people

A long time ago I learned that my happiest clients weren't always those who had the most luxurious homes or who'd achieved the greatest degree of visible success in their lives. In fact, many of the people who had 'made it' in traditional terms were the most dissatisfied.

One of the underlying reasons for this is something known as 'hedonic adaptation'. Since the 1970s, researchers have been exploring this concept, which describes our ability to make a fairly rapid adjustment to any kind of change – both positive or negative.

Studies have found that while we might be happier for a short time when we buy a new car, move into our dream home, find the perfect partner or land the promotion we've been working towards, our happiness levels return to a baseline or 'set-point' after a relatively short period of time. In the same way, when we suffer a serious accident or lose a job, there's an initial drop in happiness but in time, we might be surprised to discover that our life satisfaction is back to where we started.

Psychologists and researchers Kennon Sheldon and Sonja Lyubomirsky believe that hedonic adaptation to positive experiences occurs for two reasons. When a change occurs, such as achieving a promotion, there are positive events and positive emotions surrounding that change. You're learning new tasks, there's variety in your role, you might be earning more money, you're meeting new people and you feel proud, challenged and excited. But over time you get used to all these new things until eventually, you don't notice them anymore.

The second reason that this burst of happiness is fleeting is that you now have a 'new normal' and your aspiration level shifts upwards. In order to keep feeling satisfied, you need to keep pushing yourself in order to feel satisfied again.

My own experience and my clients' stories tells me something else, too. When we 'level up' our lives, we usually 'level up' our commitment to the new normal, and it's not always easy to come back from this.

~

My client Matt was in this position. Matt was a partner at one of the city's big consulting firms, working long hours and earning a great salary. Unfortunately, he was unhappy at work and as a result, very dissatisfied with his life.

Matt and I explored his career options, but it was clear that he had one big roadblock. His life was geared to the level of his existing income and it wasn't going to be easy to replace his salary in a different role. He had two new cars in the driveway of his home in a leafy suburb in Melbourne. His beach house was being renovated and his children were attending a prestigious private school. Many people might have looked at Matt's life and believed he had everything, but the reality was that he felt trapped and unhappy.

Despite having worked so hard for everything he had, Matt had reached a point where he would have happily given most of his material possessions away. His wife and children were happy with their lives so Matt wanted to find a compromise. We began by looking at what he could change.

# What makes a happy life?

It's up to each of us to define our own version of happiness, but it's also helpful to learn how others define contentment. Miek Wiking, founder of the Happiness Research Institute of Copenhagen, spends his days researching life satisfaction. In his book, *The Little Book of Lykke* (*lykke* means 'happiness' in Danish), Wiking identifies six important factors that make the Danes the happiest people in the world.

1. **Togetherness**
   The happiest people experience a sense of connectedness. They smile often and have good relationships with the people around them.

2. **Money**
   Wiking found that having more money doesn't necessarily make you happier but your expectations about money have an

impact on how happy you feel. Spending your money on experiences was found to be far more satisfying than spending on possessions and spending on an experience you can look forward to is one of the best ways to enjoy your money.

3. **Health**

Happy people take care of their wellbeing (eating well, exercising and getting enough sleep) but have a sense of balance about it too. Most Danes eat plenty of baked goods, for example, but they move their bodies on a daily basis, either walking or cycling to work rather than relying on cars.

4. **Freedom**

Wiking found that people who work for themselves or have a good degree of autonomy in their roles are generally happier. Happiness increased when people had time for the activities they love, and in particular, when they weren't bound by a long commute to work.

5. **Trust**

The happiest countries are those where people feel a sense of safety and security about where they live and where there's an absence of corruption in both business and politics.

6. **Kindness**

Wiking discovered that 'when we do good, we feel good'. When we find ways to make others happy through acts of kindness, we generate happiness for ourselves too.

Back in the United States, Sonja Lyubomirsky's research established that *the way we think* has a significant impact on how we view our life satisfaction.

Happy individuals view and think about events and life circumstances in more positive ways. Unhappy people spend more time dwelling on the negative aspects of events, even finding things wrong with positive events as well as ruminating about the past, while happy people are able to evaluate negative events in more positive and productive ways.

She also discovered two key elements that can help us most when it comes to avoiding hedonic adaptation.

The first is *variety* and the second is *appreciation*.

When Matt and I spoke about the hedonic adaptation findings, he realised that one of the biggest challenges in his life was the complete lack of newness or variety. His role had been much the same for 15 years, and despite the fact that he loved his family, he found his home life repetitive and, at times, even boring. He wasn't mentally stimulated in any way and as a result, he had adopted a fairly negative mindset.

Matt and I started by working on his patterns of thinking using some of the exercises outlined in the following chapters, and once he was in a slightly more positive headspace, we began to explore opportunities for him to be more creative in his personal life.

Many of the changes Matt made were minor, but the impact was significant. Instead of a long daily commute in his car, he started catching the train to make time to read. He ate lunch in several new cafes and organised a few interesting outings with his wife and their children.

The change that had the biggest impact was reconnecting with his interest in amateur acting. It was years since Matt had participated in theatre, but he pushed beyond his discomfort and joined an improv class. After overcoming his initial fear, he found a new lease of life through creative expression.

When Matt and I caught up several months later, he told me that making time for a new interest had inspired other changes too, like getting back into exercise. He felt more energised and confident and as a result, found himself speaking up more often in meetings at work. Instead of feeling trapped and resentful, Matt was now engaged and more empowered at work and much happier in his home life.

## What is going well?

It's easy to focus only on everything that's not going well in your life and to skim over or ignore the aspects that are positive. We do this because our brains have such a strong negative bias.

Before you consider what you'd like to change, take some time to reflect on the aspects of your life that are currently going well. This is one of the most immediate and effective ways to balance habitual patterns of negative thinking. It's also a useful reminder that turning our minds to the positive aspects of life can sometimes feel effortful – it's a habit we need to intentionally cultivate.

Looking at the different areas listed below, make a note of at least one thing that is going well in each area. If you're feeling somewhat dissatisfied with your life, this exercise might feel like something of a stretch, but don't stop until you've identified at least one point for each area. If you look hard enough, you'll find there's always something to be thankful for.

For example, if you're feeling unhappy because you don't have a partner at the moment, find a way to put a positive spin on your singleness in the 'Partner' category: '*I have the bathroom to myself in the mornings.*'

| Partner | |
|---|---|
| Social | |
| Family | |
| Health | |
| Career | |
| Finances | |
| Personal growth | |
| Creativity/fun | |
| Self-image | |
| Contribution to society | |

## What-went-well daily exercise

In his book *Flourish*, Dr Martin Seligman recommends a daily exercise called 'what-went-well', where you identify and write down three things that have gone well in your day and why.

Dr Seligman recommends doing this exercise every day for at least a week. His research confirmed that even six months later, the activity had significant positive effects on life satisfaction and it also reduced depression levels. Other studies on gratitude have found that the simple practice of recognising and feeling thankful for even the small elements that make life good improves our health, helps us build more positive relationships and can even extend our life span.

*For example:*

**What went well?** *I cooked a lovely dinner.*

**Why?** *I did a meal plan this week and had all the ingredients in the house which gave me more time to focus on cooking.*

**What went well?**

. . . . . . . . . . . . . . . . . . . . . . . . . . . . . . . . . . . . . . . . . . . . .

. . . . . . . . . . . . . . . . . . . . . . . . . . . . . . . . . . . . . . . . . . . . .

. . . . . . . . . . . . . . . . . . . . . . . . . . . . . . . . . . . . . . . . . . . . .

**Why?**

. . . . . . . . . . . . . . . . . . . . . . . . . . . . . . . . . . . . . . . . . . . . .

. . . . . . . . . . . . . . . . . . . . . . . . . . . . . . . . . . . . . . . . . . . . .

. . . . . . . . . . . . . . . . . . . . . . . . . . . . . . . . . . . . . . . . . . . . .

**What went well?**

. . . . . . . . . . . . . . . . . . . . . . . . . . . . . . . . . . . . . . . . . . . . . . .

. . . . . . . . . . . . . . . . . . . . . . . . . . . . . . . . . . . . . . . . . . . . . . .

. . . . . . . . . . . . . . . . . . . . . . . . . . . . . . . . . . . . . . . . . . . . . . .

**Why?**

. . . . . . . . . . . . . . . . . . . . . . . . . . . . . . . . . . . . . . . . . . . . . . .

. . . . . . . . . . . . . . . . . . . . . . . . . . . . . . . . . . . . . . . . . . . . . . .

. . . . . . . . . . . . . . . . . . . . . . . . . . . . . . . . . . . . . . . . . . . . . . .

**What went well?**

. . . . . . . . . . . . . . . . . . . . . . . . . . . . . . . . . . . . . . . . . . . . . . .

. . . . . . . . . . . . . . . . . . . . . . . . . . . . . . . . . . . . . . . . . . . . . . .

. . . . . . . . . . . . . . . . . . . . . . . . . . . . . . . . . . . . . . . . . . . . . . .

**Why?**

. . . . . . . . . . . . . . . . . . . . . . . . . . . . . . . . . . . . . . . . . . . . . . .

. . . . . . . . . . . . . . . . . . . . . . . . . . . . . . . . . . . . . . . . . . . . . . .

. . . . . . . . . . . . . . . . . . . . . . . . . . . . . . . . . . . . . . . . . . . . . . .

# TWELVE

# Learn to be mindful

*'In an age of speed, I began to think, nothing could be more invigorating than going slow. In an age of distraction, nothing can feel more luxurious than paying attention. And in an age of constant movement, nothing is more urgent than sitting still.'*

Pico Iyer

When Chris was out of work all those years ago and I was struggling to manage my anxiety, the rational part of my brain told me that the only thing I had any control over was how I dealt with the situation. So I made the decision to learn how to meditate.

It was the early 1990s and meditation wasn't popular yet in Australia. The only secular course I could find was called Transcendental Meditation (TM). I enrolled in the four-day program and, as strictly prescribed by my teacher, made the commitment to meditate twice every day for 20 minutes. It wasn't always easy to find that time with two little girls who were two and five years old, but I was determined to stick with it.

Despite my resistance to an earlier-than-already-early-morning,

I set the alarm to wake before the girls. The second meditation was squeezed in whenever I could find the time, sometimes at the end of the day before bed. Within three weeks I noticed a significant change in how I was feeling. Chris's work situation hadn't changed but the stress of it was no longer impacting me. My worries about our finances and our future receded. The toddler tantrums weren't making my chest feel as tight and I found myself able to be more present and supportive in all my relationships.

Nothing in my outer world was any different, but the way I engaged with my thoughts and our lives had completely changed. I felt a much greater capacity for equanimity and a sense of trust that things would work themselves out.

The word 'mindfulness' wasn't being used back then, but without even knowing it, I had learned to be mindful.

Jon Kabat-Zinn, who is often considered the father of mindfulness in the West, describes mindfulness as 'the awareness that arises from paying attention, on purpose, in the present moment and non-judgmentally'.

Most of us find it difficult to be truly mindful. We're often distracted by wandering thoughts about the past or future and we get caught up in self-related and often unhelpful patterns of thinking. This is what researchers call the 'default mode network' and when we're in this state of mind-wandering, we're at greater risk of anxiety and lower levels of happiness.

Mindfulness training helps us bring our attention back to our immediate experience while at the same time cultivating an attitude of kindness and acceptance towards ourselves and whatever it is we're experiencing.

For example, when you're drinking tea, you drink tea. You notice the scent, the taste, the warmth and you savour a moment of stillness. When you're in the shower, you're showering. You feel the warmth and the texture of droplets against your skin, you listen to the sound of the water and you savour the experience of showering. When you're listening to a friend, you just listen. Not wanting to jump in with your own thoughts or wanting to offer an opinion, you simply hold space for mindful listening.

Being mindful means *touching the given moment* in a purposeful way and doing your best to be with that moment without wanting to change anything. It involves momentarily quieting your discursive thinking and putting aside your preference for things to be any other way than what they are. With this open and accepting mind state, we often find that it's actually not that difficult to feel a greater sense of acceptance of our thoughts, our feelings and our lives.

We practise mindfulness by using anchors that bring us back to the present moment. The breath, the body, the senses and the ability to 'note' your experience or thoughts are just some of the ways to be mindful.

When we're *living mindfully*, we begin to see ourselves, our thoughts, our emotional reactions, our behaviours and all of our lives with greater clarity. We're able to catch ourselves when we're not in the present moment or when we're in the habit of judging. We notice when we're engaging in habitual negative thinking or escalating emotional responses.

We begin to recognise the behaviours that move us away from our values and goals and we learn to express ourselves more openly with our loved ones. We're more appreciative of the things that are going well in our lives and we move forward with life choices that feel meaningful and aligned with our values.

While a regular meditation practice is without question the most effective way to cultivate your capacity for mindfulness, there are also simple and practical ways you can be mindful in your everyday life, even when you're not meditating.

The first is to find your preferred way to come *back to the present moment.*

## Present moment exercises

Use one or more of the following suggestions to help you feel connected to the here and now. If you're new to mindfulness practice, it's usually easiest to try these methods in a quiet space before attempting to engage with them in the outside world. You might find it easiest to read through the instructions first and afterwards, practise each exercise with your eyes closed. Work up to being able to practise with open eyes and later, try the exercise in a more public space.

- Become aware of the physicality of your body and bring your awareness to where your body is in contact with the chair or the floor. Scan from the top of your head, across your forehead, around the eyes, into the jaw, across the neck and shoulders, down the arms and into the hands, across the chest and abdomen and down into the legs and feet. Can you feel the difference in different parts of your body? As you do this, you might notice parts of the body where you experience tightness or discomfort. Try to be with your experience exactly as it is initially, without trying to change anything. You might find it helpful to name what you notice, for example, 'Tightness in my jaw, openness in my chest.' Once you have an awareness of where you hold tension, you can breathe some softness into the spaces that are tight.

- Pay attention to the experience of breathing. Feel the temperature of the air as it flows in and out of your nose. Notice how your body moves as you breathe. See if you can take your in-breath into your lungs more deeply and slow your breathing down a little. You may like to pause between the in- and out-breath to help you feel more aware of your breathing. As you focus on the breath, you might notice thoughts such as, 'Am I doing this right?' Allow your mind to wander without being overly concerned about the wandering and when you notice you're distracted, gently guide your awareness back to your breath.

- Close your eyes and listen to any sounds you can hear. First, notice the sounds that are nearby and then expand your listening to take in sounds that are further away. You may notice as you listen that some sounds are more favourable than others. When we hear birdsong or a beautiful piece of music, for example, we might label these as 'good' sounds. When we hear noisy traffic, a dog barking or a baby crying, we might label these as 'bad'. Becoming aware of our inclination to judge what we hear prepares us to recognise how readily we judge all the experiences in our life as 'favourable' or 'unfavourable'. As you listen, see if you're able to label everything you hear as simply 'sounds' so that you can engage with them in a non-judgemental way. This exercise will prepare you to interact with life with a greater sense of equanimity.

- Look around your physical environment and notice everything you see. Label each object in your line of sight with a gentle matter-of-factness. 'Chair . . . table . . . trees . . . the sky . . .' and so on. Pay attention to how you feel as you look. Can you be with things, just as they are? Take the time to appreciate the objects around you without favouring them in any way.

# Be mindful of your thoughts and feelings

Once you have mastered the art of being present with your physical sensations and your environment, the next step is to become more mindful of your thoughts and feelings.

Given that we spend much of our time in 'default mode' thinking, we are often unaware that habitual thoughts and emotions can unconsciously drive our behaviours. When we start to become aware of difficult or negative thoughts, our tendency is to either overidentify with them or want to suppress them.

Being mindful doesn't mean denying our negative thoughts or feelings, nor does it mean becoming overly fixated on them.

Denial or suppression makes us feel worse and often leads to numbing behaviours. When we tell ourselves that an emotion is inappropriate or that we're being ridiculous or wrong for having it, we're essentially negating the way that we feel. When we stuff our emotions away, a cycle of unconscious escalation often begins.

Neither do we want to become overly identified with an emotion or feeling. When you say to yourself, 'I'm angry' for example, and continue to gather evidence about your rage, such as why it's justified, how someone has wronged you, etc., your whole being might become consumed with the concept of anger. In this state of mind, you're less able to see yourself, others or your experience from a balanced state of mind.

A mindful approach begins when you cultivate an open and accepting relationship with all your thoughts and feelings. From here, you can be compassionate with yourself as you have them. It's an opportunity to be curious about your experience.

When you're *identified* with the emotion of anger, you'll say to yourself, 'I'm angry', and it may feel that the feelings of anger flood your brain and your body. You're more inclined to fuel angry thoughts with additional angry thoughts, escalating feelings of anger and eventually making you more inclined to act from a place of fury.

*Suppressing* anger will sound more like, 'I shouldn't feel this way', or 'Think of all the positive aspects (of the person or experience that has triggered your anger)'. You might try to justify why you shouldn't feel angry: 'Other people have it harder than you', 'You need to get over yourself', or even, 'Anger is not a nice emotion'. The approach of suppression is actually a harsh form of self-criticism and it certainly won't energise you or make you feel stronger.

A mindful approach, on the other hand, involves recognising the first hint of anger, allowing for the emotion to be present while pausing and making a choice about how you proceed from there. When you're no longer identified with the emotion or trying to control it, rather than telling yourself, 'I'm angry', you might instead say to yourself, 'I'm noticing feelings of anger.' It's a subtle difference but try it and you'll notice that it gives you a sense of separation from your emotion. You might then find you can offer yourself compassion: 'It's normal to feel angry sometimes, and while it feels unpleasant, I can be with this feeling and still act in a mindful way.'

One of the easiest ways to catch an emotion is to return to the sensations in your body. The first hint of anger might feel like heat in your body, a racing heart, rapid breathing or tension in your muscles. If you're able to catch these responses before you act upon them, you'll have time to take a few breaths and choose how you'd like to think and behave.

People sometimes worry that allowing for difficult feelings such as sadness or grief might lead to self-pity or self-absorption or that it will send them spiralling into a deep state of depression. In something of a paradox, mindfulness research suggests that acknowledging and letting yourself feel your emotions is the first step towards accepting yourself as the imperfect but still lovable human you are and a vital step on the path to true healing.

Instead of rejecting aspects of yourself or denying your true experience, you come to recognise that there's a sense of relief that accompanies allowing for your emotions, and from this place, you can offer yourself some kindness. In time, you'll come to recognise that the strongest support you have comes from within you.

## Thoughts and feelings exercises

- Sit quietly with your eyes closed and pay close attention to your breathing. Breathe a little more deeply until you start to feel relaxed. After a few moments, see if you can be aware of what's going on in your mind. Pay attention to your most dominant thoughts. Don't be concerned if your thoughts are jumping around (this is known as 'monkey mind' and it's completely normal). Don't worry if you find that many of your thoughts are negative. Remember the brain has a natural bias in this way. Try to look at your thoughts from the perspective of a friendly observer. As best you can, just allow the thoughts to be as they are. Don't try to change them for now, just observe.

- As well as identifying patterns of thinking, ask yourself, 'How am I feeling right now?' It might surprise you to notice that you have a mix of emotions. If you're unclear about how to describe a feeling, use the following table to help you identify it. Do your best to make room for all the emotions you become aware of, rather than resisting them or trying to push them away.

### How are you feeling?

| | | | |
|---|---|---|---|
| Aggressive | Apprehensive | Acceptance | Amazed |
| Angry | Confused | Anticipation | Amused |
| Annoyed | Distracted | Aware | Appreciative |
| Anxious | Embarrassed | Calm | Delighted |
| Apathetic | Envious | Clarity | Engaged |
| Ashamed | Guilty | Connected | Excited |
| Bored | Insecure | Grateful | Fascinated |
| Depressed | Irritable | Grounded | Included |
| Disgust | Jealous | Hopeful | Joyful |
| Helpless | Overwhelmed | Peaceful | Loving |
| Hopeless | Rejected | Present | Playful |
| Lonely | Remorseful | Serene | Respected |
| Sad | Unworthy | Trusting | Valued |

- As you begin to notice your different thoughts and feelings, you might find it helpful to label them with a word or phrase. Imagine saying under your breath, 'worrying', 'planning', 'sadness', 'curiosity', 'hope', 'confusion' or whatever other words come to mind.

- Be aware of any self-criticism that arises as you notice your thoughts and feelings and remind yourself that you're experiencing the full and very normal range of human emotions. Regardless of what you're thinking or feeling, you're human and imperfect *and* still worthy of love and belonging.

- Breathe some space into the places you feel the difficult emotions most intensely and as you do this, offer yourself compassion for your experience. You might even say to yourself, 'This is difficult for me.' Allow the feelings to just be there, without feeling the need to change them in any way, and extend some kindness towards yourself.

# Be mindful of your actions

After creating greater awareness and acceptance of your thoughts and feelings, you can begin to observe how these influence your habitual behaviours too. For example, when you're experiencing sadness, you might seek solace in a tub of ice-cream or a few glasses of wine. When you're feeling irritable or angry, you might snap at the people you care about. When you're bored or lonely, you might distract yourself by scrolling through social media, binge-watching television or working long hours. These pursuits can bring immediate relief but they can also keep us from pursuing our more meaningful goals.

When you can say to yourself, 'I'm sad', 'I'm irritable', or 'I'm lonely' and offer yourself the space to feel those emotions, it becomes easier to recognise that you have a choice about how you behave.

Choosing self-kindness might result in a behaviour choice that represents genuine self-care, such as joining a yoga class, talking to a friend or taking a walk through the park. It might provide the opportunity to set a boundary in a relationship or have a difficult conversation or maybe it will be the impetus to begin the process of making more significant changes in your life.

Learning to be mindful of your actions means tuning in and aligning your choices with your values which, in turn, will set you on the path to a genuinely fulfilling life.

## Mindful of your actions exercises

Next time you find yourself heading towards one of your unhelpful behavioural habits, try catching your thoughts and feelings before acting on them.

- Meditate. Meditation is one of the most helpful ways to create an intentional 'pause' before you behave in a habitual way. You'll find simple instructions on page 112 at the end of this chapter.

- Get to know your preferred ways of numbing or escaping difficult feelings. Without judging yourself harshly, tune in to the behaviours that might seem comforting in the immediate moment but that actually deplete you overall. Some of the common ones are overeating, excessive alcohol consumption, using illicit or prescription drugs or the overuse of online shopping, social media, television or gaming. You may find that you also use more socially acceptable ways of numbing such as overworking, overexercising or taking care of others at the expense of yourself.

- Make a list of activities that provide genuine comfort or that are more supportive of your wellbeing. When you find yourself wanting to numb your feelings in unhelpful ways, choose one of these activities instead.

# Be compassionate

As you start to become more mindful of your thoughts, feelings and behaviours, it's likely that you'll be more aware of the tendency to be hard on yourself, and you might also notice that the inclination to judge yourself leads to judging others too.

Letting go of judgement is perhaps the most difficult aspect of mindfulness. In Western culture, we're conditioned to measure ourselves against our peers. If during your school years you weren't gifted academically or artistically and you didn't have a talent for sport, it's possible you felt that you were lacking in some way. If you had the misfortune of being bullied in the schoolyard, you may still carry some of those wounds with you today.

Our early experiences shape the way we interact with ourselves and they influence the way we feel in relation to other people. If you were lucky enough to have mostly positive experiences during your younger years, you're more likely to perceive the world as a friendly, hospitable place. But if, like many of my clients, you encountered challenging relationships at home or at school, it's likely that your 'threat' system has become overly vigilant when it comes to measuring yourself against the people around you.

Cultivating compassion is one of the most helpful ways to minimise judgement. As well as engaging the soothing part of your brain, research tells us that compassion can help you feel more positive, hopeful and resilient, and lower your stress levels. It also helps create empathy, giving us the opportunity for deeper connection in all our relationships.

Practising compassion for others is easiest when we're able to be compassionate towards ourselves. You'll learn how to do this in the following chapter but first, try the following techniques to help you cultivate compassion towards the people around you.

## Compassion exercises

- Approach all your interactions over the next 24 hours from a place of kindness. As best you can, set aside judgement and greet people with an open heart. Notice the difference both in how it feels and how people respond to you.
- When you encounter someone who is being difficult, imagine you can sense that beneath their prickliness is some kind of pain. Abrasive people are dealing with their own difficult emotions too.
- Rather than subscribing to rigid ideas about people who are different from you, become curious about differences in culture, race and religion. Find out why people have certain ideas or opinions rather than immediately jumping to critical judgement.
- Consider how you would like to be treated if you were going through adversity and treat others with the same kindness and respect you would hope to receive.

- When you find yourself in the midst of conflict, say to yourself, 'This is a difficult conversation for both of us,' rather than focusing solely on being right.

# Make life plans mindfully

Living mindfully means making *conscious* choices about your life. It involves bringing your awareness back to your values and strengths and committing to living with purpose.

- Revisit Chapter 4 (page 22) to review your values and consider how aligned you currently are with each of those values.
- Revisit the exercise where you identified the best possible version of yourself on pages 57–8.
- Review your current strengths from the exercise in Chapter 5 (page 39) and consider which of these strengths really makes you feel alive.
- Think about what you would love to be doing to make a difference in the world (whether it's connected to your work or not).
- Review your five-year vision (Chapter 8, pages 66–7). If you haven't written your vision statement, set aside an afternoon to daydream about your version of a meaningful life. Write in the present tense and cover as many areas as you can.
- As you begin to pursue your plans, mindfully check in from time to time that your choices are right for you and not just those that will look good to the outside world or those that will please others.

# Learn to meditate

Contrary to what many people think, meditation and mindfulness are not the same things. While you do need to be mindful in order to meditate, you don't need to engage in a formal meditation practice in order to be mindful in your everyday life. But a regular meditation practice really is the most effective way to cultivate the skill of becoming more aware.

If you're new to meditation, it's generally easiest to learn by enrolling in a class. Rather than concerning yourself with which style of meditation is best (the best form is the one you'll commit to), find a teacher and a practice you connect with.

If you want to learn from the comfort of your own home, try the free meditation course or some of the beginner's meditations on the Insight Timer app.

Following are instructions for a simple breath meditation to get you started. Read the instructions right through before you begin.

- Find a comfortable place to meditate, where you won't be interrupted for 15–20 minutes, and switch off all devices. Sit in a comfy chair rather than lying down so you don't fall asleep. Close your eyes and take a few breaths, in and out through your nose.

- Start by paying attention to all aspects of your breathing without changing your breath in any way. Feel the breath as it enters the nose. Notice how the body moves as you breathe. Notice the temperature of the breath as it passes across the top lip, notice the sound of the breath and notice how your body moves as you breathe. Observe all the different sensations that make up the experience of breathing.

- Next, follow the path of the breath as it enters the nose, passes into the throat and the lungs. Follow the breath as it leaves your body. Continue like this for the rest of your meditation.
- As you try to keep your attention on the breath, it's completely natural for your mind to wander. When thoughts arise, gently let them go as you guide your attention back to your breath.
- It's also completely normal to feel like you are not 'doing it right' or not feeling any change in your experience. This is a normal part of the practice. While some people do feel more deeply relaxed during their meditation, it's also common to experience boredom or restlessness or to feel a desire for a sense of enlightenment. For most people, the benefits of meditation are felt as a cumulative effect of a regular practice.
- Remember that the intention of meditation isn't to seek 'nothingness' or an empty mind. Your aim is to simply do your best to focus your attention on one thing at a time. When your mind wanders, direct it back to the breath. When you are distracted by something (such as noise or thoughts), allow the distraction to be a reminder to go deeper into your meditation.
- Continue like this for at least five minutes, or if you're comfortable, for up to 20 minutes. If you're concerned about timing your practice, use the timer on the Insight Timer app at the beginning of your meditation, and set it to sound a chime when the practice is finished.
- At the end of your meditation, sit for a few minutes before resuming your normal activities.
- Ideally, commit to a daily meditation practice for at least three weeks before making any judgement about whether you're benefiting.

# Beginning to be mindful

Create a few 'touchpoints' in your day when you can remember to bring your awareness back to the present moment. For example, take a few breaths upon waking or before drinking your first cup of tea. Engage your senses fully while enjoying your morning coffee. Become more aware of how you carry your body when you're exercising. Tune in to your emotions as you close your laptop at the end of the day. Each of these practices will help cultivate greater awareness of your inner experience, while at the same time making you more aware of living fully in the present moment.

**When will you remember to be more present?**

# THIRTEEN

# Practise self-compassion

*'A moment of self-compassion can change your entire day. A string of such moments can change the course of your life.'*

Christopher K. Germer

Mel worked in a high-pressure role as an executive assistant to a partner in a city law firm. Her work was demanding, well paid and she performed it exceptionally well. She had a family she loved and a great group of friends but when she came to see me, she felt flat and lonely.

'I think I'll just throw it all in and go to Bali to do yoga teacher training,' she told me. Which sounded like a lovely idea, but she also acknowledged that this wasn't entirely realistic. She was single and in her late forties, with a large credit card debt, little super, no assets and no plan for her future financial wellbeing.

We agreed that it might be worth her chatting to a financial advisor before making any dramatic change and meanwhile, we'd do some work on improving her overall happiness. Mel shared that she'd been lonely for a long time and she spent money whenever she felt flat. She bought beautiful clothes, expensive dinners and took luxury holidays to 'treat herself'.

She knew that the pain she was trying to mask wasn't soothed by spending. Beneath her stylish exterior was a woman who felt embarrassed about her lack of financial security and who was in a perpetual cycle of being critical of herself, spending money, feeling guilty and becoming more self-critical. Not wanting her vulnerability to be seen by others, Mel had never revealed the truth of her financial situation or her ongoing stress to anyone. None of her friends would have guessed that this was a woman who was not only financially exposed, but who found her situation increasingly anxiety-provoking.

Like most self-critical people, Mel's feelings of unworthiness, guilt and shame were clouding her ability to find a more effective way to soothe herself. We started by working on Mel's relationship with herself.

Having recently completed a Mindful Self-Compassion training program and feeling the full benefits of this approach myself, I introduced Mel to the work of Kristin Neff, professor of psychology at the University of Texas and a leading researcher in self-compassion.

Self-compassion is the practice that allows us to extend kindness towards ourselves, particularly during times of difficulty. While it's not quite an antidote to self-criticism, self-compassion helps us to be with our painful experiences in a more mindful and open way.

Instead of turning against ourselves and being our own worst critics, self-compassion helps us to speak to ourselves with the same kind of understanding and support we would offer a good friend.

It helps us to become more accepting of our imperfections and allows us to be gentle with ourselves, rather than angry when we fall short in some way.

One of the great myths of self-compassion is that it will make you self-absorbed or self-indulgent. Nothing could be further from the truth. In fact, when you take care of your own emotional and physical needs, you have more love, empathy and understanding to offer to the people around you, while also being better equipped to take care of yourself during difficult times.

Scientific studies suggest there are physical benefits to practising compassion, too. It increases DHEA, a hormone that counteracts the ageing process, and reduces the stress hormone cortisol. It makes us feel good, it makes others feel good, and it's good for our longevity.

Kristin Neff suggests that self-compassion involves three core elements: self-kindness, common humanity and mindfulness.

## Self-kindness vs self-judgement

When you practise self-kindness, you extend the same kind wishes to yourself that you would offer a good friend who was going through a tough time. Instead of criticising yourself or trying to force away your feelings, you remind yourself that it's human to be imperfect and that each of us will experience emotions such as loneliness, sadness, frustration, anxiety and anger at times. We'll all make errors, mistakes and misjudgements. Instead of exacerbating negative feelings by telling yourself how flawed you are, the message you tell yourself is, 'I made a mistake', not 'I am a mistake'.

Try the following exercises to help cultivate the practice of self-kindness. They might feel strange or weird at first, but it's worth noting that these concepts are well researched and they're designed to make you more resilient and self-sufficient.

## Offer yourself words of comfort

Remind yourself that *all* human beings are worthy of love and belonging. Next time you find yourself feeling unworthy, tell yourself that you are as valuable as anyone by repeating this mantra: 'Despite the fact that I . . . (yelled at my kids / had a fight with my partner / made a mistake at work / don't get on with my brother, etc.), I am still a person who is worthy of love and belonging.'

## Soothing touch

Try offering yourself 'soothing touch', a practice that helps engage the parasympathetic nervous system to bring down the stress response. Place one or both hands on your heart area and feel the warmth and pressure of touch on your chest. You may find it soothing to make small circling movements with your hands. Repeat a soothing phrase in the same way you would offer words of kindness to a friend. For example, 'I'm here for you,' or 'I understand you.'

## Self-compassion letter

Write a letter to yourself, from the perspective of a compassion-ate, caring friend. Imagine this friend accepts you unconditionally, including the aspects of yourself that are imperfect. This friend is someone who is kind and forgiving and they understand how your life experiences have contributed to making you who you are today. As you write your letter from their perspective, imagine how they would convey love, acceptance and generosity towards you, and in particular, towards the parts of yourself that you find most difficult to accept. After writing the letter, put it aside for a while and when you come back to read it, allow the compassion to really sink in.

Most people find it helpful to repeat the letter-writing (and reading) exercises several times over a few months.

## This is a moment of suffering

As you encounter difficult feelings, say to yourself:

- This is a moment of suffering.
- Suffering is part of life; I am not alone in my suffering.
- May I be kind to myself, may I give myself what I need.

# Common humanity vs isolation

When we encounter difficult emotions, we sometimes think we are the only ones who feel this way. It helps to remember that everyone experiences emotional pain at times and we all make mistakes. We all have regrets, we encounter setbacks in life and at times we compare ourselves unfavourably to others.

When we remind ourselves that we're not alone in our suffering, we become less judgemental of our errors and more forgiving of ourselves, which, in turn, makes us more accepting of and more willing to forgive the flaws in others.

Recognising the shared experience of suffering also helps us to feel less isolated. Even the simple act of taking a few breaths and saying to yourself, 'At this very moment, there are literally thousands of others around the world who are experiencing the same kind of emotional pain as me,' helps to create some perspective and makes you feel less alone.

Rather than focusing on differences, focus on what you have in common with others. We all need food, shelter and love. We all crave attention, understanding, affection and happiness. We hope to achieve, to be recognised and to feel valued for who we are.

## Just like me

Bring to mind someone you care about who you know has experienced adversity recently. If you're feeling generous, you might like to think of a person you've had an unpleasant encounter with. As you bring that person into your awareness, repeat the following phrases, ideally saying them out loud, replacing 'this person' with their name.

- 'Just like me, this person is seeking happiness in their life.'
- 'Just like me, this person is trying to avoid suffering in their life.'
- 'Just like me, this person has known sadness, loneliness and despair.'
- 'Just like me, this person is seeking to fill their needs.'
- 'Just like me, this person is learning about life.'

## Tonglen meditation

Tonglen meditation is a Tibetan Buddhist meditation dating back to the 11th century that helps to awaken compassion for others. It is a practice also known as the 'giving and taking' or 'sending and receiving' meditation. The goal of the practice is to help you to overcome your aversion to other people's suffering (which, in turn, will help you to overcome the aversion to your own suffering), to remind you of the connectedness of all beings, and to awaken in you the compassion to help others.

If you're new to self-compassion, you may find it helpful to listen to a guided Loving Kindness meditation before practising Tonglen. You'll find a Loving Kindness meditation of mine on the free Insight Timer app.

To practise Tonglen, close your eyes and connect to a feeling of stillness. Take a few deep breaths to help open your heart. Imagine now that as you breathe in, you become aware of any of the difficult emotions you carry within you. Imagine that as the energy passes through your heart area with the in-breath, those emotions are cleansed and renewed. As you breathe out, the energy is lighter and more positive.

Next, think of someone you care about who is suffering in some way. As you breathe in, imagine you're able to breathe in their difficulty, along with a wish to end their suffering. Breathe out love, compassion and kindness and imagine that your intention helps relieve them of pain.

As you do this practice, continue to pay attention to your own negative emotions too, and imagine that you're breathing in for all the people who are caught in the same emotions as yours.

Breathe in for all who are suffering and breathe out offering comfort and healing and freedom from pain.

Tonglen can be done for those who are in discomfort of any kind. It can be done as a formal meditation practice or you can use it during your day when you encounter someone who is being difficult or when you recognise another person's discomfort or pain.

You may find that you can mentally offer the words, 'I'm sorry for your suffering,' to yourself and to others. This may help to ease some discomfort.

The Tonglen practice might initially sound unappealing given that it infers that you take on other people's pain, but it actually helps us to understand that much of our suffering comes from resisting difficult emotions. When we are able to open our hearts and make room for our own difficulty, and other people's, we discover a deep sense of connection with our fellow human beings and those feelings of connection offer us access to the infinite capacity for healing that exists within all of us.

## Mindfulness vs overidentification

Being mindful of our experience rather than being overidentified with it means acknowledging and accepting our shortcomings, our negative emotions and our mistakes (and subsequently, ourselves) in a loving and non-judgemental way. As we reflected earlier in the mindfulness chapter (page 98), we neither ignore nor suppress our difficult emotions, nor do we exaggerate or escalate them.

Being aware, in the moment, of our thoughts and feelings helps us to accept them for what they are.

Instead of ruminating or catastrophising, if we are able to mentally step back from our thoughts and say to ourselves, 'This is what I'm noticing,' we come to recognise that we have choices about how we feel and how we behave going forward.

## Catch your habitual self-talk

Choose one difficult thought that you have on a regular basis and become aware of your typical self-talk and the accompanying emotions. For example, 'I'm not as healthy / sociable / confident / intelligent as I should be.' Notice how you feel when you have that thought and name those feelings. 'I feel unattractive / disappointed in myself / filled with self-loathing / like a failure.'

When you notice these painful thoughts and feelings, instead of engaging in your usual patterns of thinking or your habitual ways of trying to numb the accompanying feelings, change your self-talk to something more compassionate such as, 'I'm being really hard on myself here.'

## Be with your feelings

As you go through your days, try to catch yourself as you have your most common negative thoughts and feelings. Notice when you have the expectation that you should only experience positive emotions and instead of resisting the more challenging emotions, allow yourself to feel your pain. Say to yourself, 'I can be with these feelings. They're just feelings and they'll pass,' and at the same time, send some kindness your own way.

Mel found the self-compassion work transformative. Her self-critical thoughts about her financial situation had made her unwilling to open up to her friends, making her feel even more isolated and stressed.

She realised that she had been quick to numb her emotional needs with spending, instead of acknowledging her vulnerability with kindness and offering herself internal support.

After offering herself the practices of *words of comfort* and *soothing touch* over several months, Mel developed a more accepting relationship with herself, and over time, she found she was comfortable to be more open with her friends.

Learning to be kind to yourself takes time – possibly even years – but as Mel found (and as I have discovered in my own life, too), when you change the relationship you have with yourself, you discover that there's a whole different way of living in this world.

# FOURTEEN

# Make room for your difficult thoughts and feelings

*'The primary cause of unhappiness is never the situation, but your thoughts about it.'*

Eckhart Tolle

Acceptance and Commitment Therapy (also known as 'ACT') is a form of therapy that teaches us to deal with our difficult thoughts and feelings in a more mindful way. This habit can help us to create more fulfilling lives and we can do this even when we have the experience of some internal discomfort.

ACT makes the assumption that we will all encounter challenging thoughts and emotions as an innate and ongoing part of life. Alongside these emotional experiences, we can still live in alignment with our values and, in turn, create rich, full and meaningful lives.

As ACT expert Russ Harris suggests, *your mind is not your friend or your enemy* but rather, it's a complex set of processes that include analysing, imagining, perceiving, evaluating, visualising, planning, comparing, appreciating, remembering and deciding.

Thinking can be both *positive* and *negative*, but if we don't learn to manage our thoughts effectively, they can cause us pain at any time.

Throughout our lives we're all going to experience joy, laughter and love, but we'll also face moments of self-doubt, anxiety, sadness and grief. When we encounter difficult emotions, we can become 'fused' with our thoughts and this is when we're more likely to get overly caught up in repetitive negative patterns of thinking. At such times, we're inclined to be critical of ourselves and others, to rehash painful memories, and we might even start to imagine unpleasant futures.

When negative thinking becomes a habit, your mind has the power to interrupt even your happiest moments with self-critical thoughts. Unchecked, these patterns of thinking can even lead to self-destructive or self-limiting behaviours.

As we learned in the earlier chapter on mindfulness (page 103), ACT therapists also take the view that most psychological suffering is caused by our desire to *escape* or *avoid* the thoughts and feelings that cause us pain.

It might seem counterintuitive to believe that opening up to and allowing your difficult emotional experiences will free you from suffering, but when you look at the strategies you currently engage to avoid your pain, it's likely you'll see that they haven't been working.

ACT calls these 'emotional control strategies'. They include the numbing behaviours we touched on earlier. While many of these strategies are relatively harmless in small doses and they may even offer relief in the short-term, in the longer term, they can escalate, causing practical problems and adding to our emotional pain. These strategies can often get in the way of doing things that matter to us, like living in alignment with our values.

ACT is an invitation for us to learn to be with the difficult emotions we experience. Using this form of therapy doesn't mean you *want* to feel the pain, it means you're *willing* to, in service of doing what matters and being the person you want to be.

A few months into her new relationship with Sam, my client Lily was facing her own experience of difficult emotions. Sam was kind and funny and considerate but because she'd been hurt by two previous partners, Lily found it hard to trust that this new relationship would last. She spent a lot of time feeling fearful and anxious and questioning why someone like Sam would be interested in her.

Lily found it difficult to be present when she was with Sam. Her mind was so busy worrying that she came across as distracted and at times, even uninterested. This was exacerbated when they were in the company of other people.

One Sunday afternoon, Lily and Sam joined a few of Sam's friends for a picnic. The group went out of their way to make her feel welcome and Lily was doing her best to relax. But she found it difficult to engage in the conversation because her mind was busy making comparisons between herself and the other girls in the group. They appeared confident and outgoing and at ease with themselves. Lily felt self-conscious and dull and at a loss for anything to say.

Because she was so caught up in her self-criticism, Lily wasn't able to interact in a meaningful way. Her thoughts were clouding her ability to be present, and as the afternoon progressed, she felt more unhappy and ill at ease.

ACT focuses on two main areas – developing acceptance of our private thoughts and committing to actions that move us towards a valued life.

There are six key processes that work together to help with this. When Lily and I met over the coming weeks, we worked through the processes together.

## 1. Contact the present moment

When Lily and I spoke about the picnic, she could see that she'd been so caught up in self-judgement that she wasn't able to listen to or engage in the group's conversation. She recognised that this was a pattern of hers, not just when she was with other people but when she was working, reading, eating – she was so often caught up in anxious thoughts that she was rarely in the present moment. Almost always when she was in company, her mind went into an autopilot mode of comparing herself to others.

Lily's homework was to find one way each day to bring herself back to the present moment. She agreed that she would start with the relatively easy task of eating her breakfast mindfully before trying to be more mindful in other areas of her life. This meant sitting down and eating without reading or watching television or distracting herself in any other way. As she ate, she would really taste each mouthful and she'd also be aware of the thoughts and feelings that were present. After breakfast, Lily was going to make a few notes in her journal that she would share with me in a subsequent session.

When we met the following week, Lily was surprised at how much she had enjoyed the taste of the food she'd eaten, but she had also become aware of how frequent her negative thoughts were. Lily decided that she would spend the next few weeks trying to observe (without trying to change) her habitual patterns of negative thinking.

## 2. Defusion

The aim of 'defusion' is to give us the opportunity to step back from unhelpful thoughts so that we might see them for what they really are. Many are judgements, opinions, memories or simply unhelpful thinking habits that have developed over time. When we're able to distance ourselves from such thoughts we often see that despite the fact that they're not necessarily believable, we let these thoughts frighten or disturb us and they sometimes control our behaviour.

Defusion means being able to step back and label your thoughts as 'thinking'. Instead of being swept up by them or struggling to get rid of them, you *allow* thoughts to come and go, in much the same way as you observe the weather coming and going. Some days are stormy and dark, while others are peaceful and clear. We know we can't control the weather, in the same way that we can't easily control our thoughts, but we do know that even the most wild storm eventually passes.

There are many different ways to practise defusion. Lily found it easiest to do this by naming the thoughts she was having – 'self-criticism', 'judgement', 'worrying', 'comparing' and saying to herself, 'My mind is telling me the story that I'm not good enough.'

## 3. Acceptance

As Lily started to label her thoughts, she also became aware of the emotions that accompanied those thoughts and discovered that *fear* was a recurring theme for her. She was fearful of other people's opinions of her, fearful of not measuring up, fearful of losing Sam and even fearful of feeling anxious. As she connected with the emotion of fear, she also became aware that she felt this mostly as a tightness in her chest.

In our next session, I asked Lily to close her eyes and describe that sensation of fear as though from the perspective of a curious scientist. Instead of trying to change it or wanting it to go away, she looked at the sensation of fear with an open mind. She saw it as a ball of tension in her chest and described the shape, the weight and the colour of the sensation of fear.

I asked her to take a couple of deep breaths into her chest space, not trying to change the fear or make it go away but simply making room for her experience and allowing the emotion to be there (even though she didn't like how it felt). Next, I invited Lily to breathe a bit of openness and space around the sensation of fear saying, under her breath, 'allowing, allowing'. Between our sessions, she agreed to continue this simple guided meditation.

When you're able to drop the struggle and give your thoughts and their accompanying emotions some space in your body, you often find that it's easier for feelings to come and go more readily.

## 4. The observing self

There are two parts to the mind – the *thinking self* and the *observing self*. The *thinking self* is automatic and it tells you many stories about yourself. Some are neutral ('I'm an artist', 'I am walking'), others are positive ('I'm generous', 'I feel happy today') and many are critical ('I'm socially awkward', 'I'm depressed').

The *observing self* is able to see that thinking is made up of two aspects: the thinking itself, and your observation of thoughts. When we're able to observe our thinking, we can be less judgemental of our thoughts and recognise that while we *think our thoughts*, we are not the *thoughts themselves*. In this way, we can see that our internal experiences are no longer threatening or controlling.

As Lily stepped back from her habitual patterns of thinking, she was able to engage in what we call 'pure awareness'. Watching her difficult thoughts from this perspective, she could also observe her feelings of fear and anxiety with compassion. She was able to see that even when these difficult thoughts and feelings were present, she could still align her actions with her values.

## 5. Values

One of Lily's highest values was 'connection'. Through her experience with ACT, she learned that being fused with negative thoughts and fixated on fear made it difficult for her to create connection. She also recognised that it was impossible to enjoy a pleasant activity such as an outing with Sam's friends when she was caught up in comparing herself to others.

Lily and I revisited her values and reflected on the words she had chosen. As well as her value of connection, Lily valued independence, creativity, love, compassion, kindness, openness, acceptance, curiosity and authenticity.

Connecting with her deepest values helped Lily to recognise that she wasn't really interested in being like other people – she cared mostly about being true to herself. She was open to people who were different from her, so in the same way that she could offer kindness, compassion and acceptance to other people, Lily began to explore how she could offer these qualities to herself.

## 6. Committed action

Lily made a commitment to be fully engaged in her next conversation with Sam. Instead of worrying about herself or planning her responses, she did her best to just listen. She tuned in when her mind was wandering and brought herself back to being present.

At their next outing with friends, Lily was able to catch herself when she wasn't listening and when she had started comparing herself with one of Sam's friends. Internally, she was quickly able to label the thought 'comparing' while turning her attention back to the conversation.

Over the coming months, Lily began to feel a deeper sense of connection with Sam and his friendship group. There were still times when she was distracted by negative thoughts, but for the most part she was able to bring together the elements of ACT to meet the present moment with awareness, openness and meaning.

## An easy way to remember ACT

The acronym ACT encapsulates the entire model and helps us to remember the steps in difficult moments.

A = Accept your thoughts and feelings, and be present.

C = Choose a valued direction.

T = Take action.

## When you're overly anxious

Long before ACT was a form of therapy, an Australian scientist, Claire Weekes, was fighting her own battle with anxiety that would lead her to a form of treatment that is not dissimilar to ACT.

It was the late 1920s and Weekes had a long-standing issue with a palpitating heart. Incorrectly diagnosed with tuberculosis and having spent six months in a sanatorium without improvement, Weekes was convinced she had a serious heart condition.

A chance conversation with a colleague gave Weekes an insight into what was causing her condition. What she later called 'the habit of fear', was a self-perpetuating cycle where stress and anxiety were feeding on themselves to evoke her body's fight–flight response. Weekes recognised that her palpitating heart was caused by her fear of fear itself. This finding would transform the way she dealt with her anxiety and would lead her to develop a thoughtful approach to managing anxiety with others.

Weekes discovered that when she stopped engaging in the experience of fear so intensely and stopped *fighting* her racing heart, her condition improved quickly. Piqued by her interest in her 'nerves', she began practising as a doctor in Sydney where she saw patients with a whole range of ailments related to panic or anxiety disorders. Her prescription was *acceptance of fear*.

Weekes created a treatment plan that comprised six words: *face, accept, float, let time pass*. Like ACT, the objective wasn't to eradicate anxious feelings but rather to help people find a different way to interact with their discomfort.

Claire Weekes understood that encouraging her patients to fully experience their panic, rather than resist it, allowed the experience to 'pass through' to the other side.

# FIFTEEN

# Overcome your irrational beliefs

*'You find peace not by rearranging the circumstances of your life, but by realising who you are at the deepest level.'*

Eckhart Tolle

Aoife came to talk with me about returning to work after having her children. She had left a leadership role in the public service three years earlier, just before her son was born, and now with her second son about to turn one, she wasn't feeling confident to return to her role.

The biggest obstacle she faced was internal – she couldn't envisage doing a good job of parenting *and* returning to work. Her standards at home and at work were high (in her own words, she was something of a perfectionist) and whenever she began to think about work, all she could focus on was how being a parent was going to limit her capacity to perform her role well.

Aoife and I spent some time exploring her belief system.

～

135

Midway through the last century, the American psychologist Albert Ellis studied how our thoughts and beliefs play a part in our psychological wellbeing. He believed that we all hold a set of assumptions about ourselves, about others and about our lives that influence how we think about and respond to life events.

Ellis discovered that many of these assumptions are inherently negative and irrational. These 'irrational beliefs' appeared to lead to behaviours that inhibited happiness.

According to Ellis, an irrational belief is one that:

- Distorts reality
- Is illogical
- Prevents you from reaching your goals
- Leads to unhealthy emotion
- Leads to self-sabotaging behaviour

Like many other researchers, Ellis believed that the way we *feel* is largely influenced by how we *think*, and when we become fixated on our irrational beliefs, our feelings lead to behaviours that inhibit the achievement of our goals.

Ellis created a form of therapy called Rational Emotive Behaviour Therapy (REBT) which works on the assumption that if we recognise our beliefs and identify those that are irrational, we can challenge them. When we're able to alter the way we interpret events, we can also alter our behaviour.

In order to challenge your irrational beliefs, you need to begin by identifying those beliefs – and then you need to dispute them.

Most irrational beliefs fall into one of three categories. Ellis called these the *Three Major Musts*.

# The Three Major Musts

1. **Beliefs about yourself:**
   *I must do well and win the love and approval of others. If I fail,*
   *I am an unworthy person who deserves to suffer.*
   This belief places unrealistic expectations on yourself, shows
   an overconcern with other people's opinions of you, equates
   self-worth with achievement and demonstrates a lack of self-
   acceptance.

   It can lead to self-criticism, anxiety, depression, avoiding risk,
   perfectionism, overworking and a lack of assertiveness.

2. **Beliefs about others:**
   *The people I associate with must treat me fairly, must not criticise*
   *me, they must be competent and live up to their own potential.*
   This belief places unrealistic expectations on others. It makes
   the assumption that there's a clear difference between right and
   wrong, and human fallibility is not acceptable.

   This belief can lead to feelings of impatience, anger, blame,
   resentment and intolerance.

3. **Beliefs about the world:**
   *Life must be safe, easy, enjoyable and fair and if it's not, it's hardly*
   *worth living.*
   This belief overestimates our right to a trouble-free life and makes
   the assumption that our lives should be free from adversity.

   It can lead to feelings of entitlement, self-pity, anxiety and
   depression and an overindulgence in 'feel-good' behaviours
   such as overeating or indulging in alcohol or drugs, as well as
   procrastination or avoiding responsibility in life.

In my first few sessions with Aoife, we began to explore her irrational beliefs. Most of her concerns fell within the first of the Major Musts. For as long as she could remember, Aoife had felt pressure to be perfect. This came partly from her high-achieving parents and the comparisons she made between herself and her older sister, but it was also the way Aoife related to herself.

Aoife shared that even in her primary school days, she had held the expectation that she needed to be good at everything. Despite being above average in her academic abilities, Aoife was critical of herself for not *always* being the A+ student her sister was.

By the time she reached the workforce, her desire to appear perfect made her a workaholic. She put herself under pressure to perform to the highest possible standard. Her internal message that 'I must be perfect always' also meant she was inclined towards a form of black-and-white thinking – if she wasn't 'good', she was 'bad'. If she couldn't complete a task at work in the expected time frame, she was inadequate in her role.

She applied the same pressure to her motherhood role. If she lost her temper with her children, she was a bad mother. If she had a day where she wasn't enjoying the children, she felt that there was something wrong with her.

Albert Ellis believed that irrational thinking is something all of us do from time to time, but when we become overly fixated on a Major Must, it inhibits our wellbeing. He discovered that we can overcome the frequency and intensity of those thoughts by disputing our irrational beliefs.

# Dispute your Major Musts

Once you know your Major Musts, you can ask yourself a series of questions about whether those beliefs are entirely true. Instead of feeling that the belief is set in stone, you might find that you can replace an irrational belief with one that infers that it's a preference, rather than a 'must'.

For example:

1. 'My preference is to perform well in most areas of my life and for others to approve of me, but I know this won't always be the case. Even if I fail sometimes, I know that I'm a good person.'
2. 'My preference is to be treated kindly and with love, but because I'm not in control of other people's behaviour and because it's normal for all people to make mistakes, I understand that this won't be the case all the time.'
3. 'My preference is for life to be safe and fair and easy and I acknowledge that it's frustrating when it isn't, but I can accept that like everyone else, I will encounter adversity from time to time.'

Ellis's ABCDE model helps us to understand how our beliefs, feelings and behaviour are connected. The model works in the following way.

## A – Activating event
An event occurs that leads to a negative or highly emotional response. For Aoife, an example of this was recalling a mistake she'd made at work just before going on maternity leave.

## B – Beliefs

Your thoughts and interpretations of the event are based on your beliefs. In Aoife's case, her belief that 'I should be perfect at my job' led to the interpretation that her single mistake meant she had lost her edge.

## C – Consequences

As a consequence of your beliefs, you feel certain emotions about the event and those emotions lead you to certain behaviours. Aoife's emotions were embarrassment, shame and later, anxiety about losing her job (even though she knew this thought was irrational). These feelings made it more difficult to focus at work and harder to feel at ease with her manager.

Once the ABCs are discovered and explored, the intervention (DE) begins.

## D – Dispute

Next, we dispute or challenge the dysfunctional beliefs.

- Is this belief really true?
- What evidence is there?

Aoife started to challenge her belief by asking, 'Do I really need to be perfect? Does making one mistake mean that I'm totally inadequate?'

Here are some other ways to dispute a belief:

- Am I exaggerating or overemphasising a negative aspect of the situation?
- Am I catastrophising or making things worse than they really are?

- Is this thinking helping me to achieve my goals?
- Does it help me foster healthy and happy relationships?
- What would I say to a friend in this situation?
- Is there another way to look at this situation?

When you're able to examine your beliefs in this way, you also begin to understand that there are other ways to think.

For example:

- At a rational level, I know that no one is perfect. Everyone makes mistakes at times.
- I am exaggerating this. It's an error that can be fixed and I'll be better able to do that when I'm not fixated on negative thoughts.
- My emotional reaction is creating distance between me and my colleagues and manager.
- This thinking is costing me emotional energy with no benefit in return.

## E – Effect

This is the effect or consequence of challenging your unhelpful beliefs. If you're able to change a 'must' statement to a 'preference', it's likely that you'll see the situation with greater clarity and without the distortion of irrational thinking.

It didn't take Aoife long to arrive at a more balanced way of thinking. 'I don't have to be perfect in everything I do. I've learned from the mistake I made and I won't make it again. I'd prefer to never make mistakes but if I can be grounded and calm about that one error, I can return to work and enjoy performing well in my role.'

It's helpful to keep in mind that while the ABCDE model is aimed at challenging irrational beliefs, it's not about denying normal emotions such as sadness, anger, hurt, regret, grief and even realistic fears. These emotions will be present at different times in our lives and we want to interact with these in a mindful and self-compassionate way.

When we take this balanced approach, it becomes easier to see when you're escalating a problem rather than having a healthy, human response to it.

## Cultivate acceptance

Another of the goals of REBT is to help us develop a greater level of acceptance of reality, even when our experiences are less than pleasant. Use the following phrases (or write out adaptations of them in your own words) to cultivate a more balanced way of thinking.

**Unconditional self-acceptance:** I have positive and negative aspects of myself and like everyone, I'm a fallible human being. Even with my imperfections, I am worthy of love and belonging.

**Unconditional other-acceptance:** Other people will treat me unfairly sometimes and even the people who love me most will appear unloving at times. There's no reason why they have to treat me well all the time and even when they're imperfect, they're no less worthy of love and belonging than I am.

**Unconditional life-acceptance:** Life won't always go as I would like it to. I acknowledge that it will be a mix of uncertainty, change, suffering and joy. I can accept the difficult days along with the good ones.

# Challenge your irrational beliefs

Review the list of Major Musts on page 137 and identify your most commonly held irrational beliefs. Make a note of them below.

. . . . . . . . . . . . . . . . . . . . . . . . . . . . . . . . . . . . . . . . . . . .

. . . . . . . . . . . . . . . . . . . . . . . . . . . . . . . . . . . . . . . . . . . .

. . . . . . . . . . . . . . . . . . . . . . . . . . . . . . . . . . . . . . . . . . . .

. . . . . . . . . . . . . . . . . . . . . . . . . . . . . . . . . . . . . . . . . . . .

**How do your irrational beliefs hold you back from living a fulfilling life?**

. . . . . . . . . . . . . . . . . . . . . . . . . . . . . . . . . . . . . . . . . . . .

. . . . . . . . . . . . . . . . . . . . . . . . . . . . . . . . . . . . . . . . . . . .

. . . . . . . . . . . . . . . . . . . . . . . . . . . . . . . . . . . . . . . . . . . .

. . . . . . . . . . . . . . . . . . . . . . . . . . . . . . . . . . . . . . . . . . . .

**Use the ABCDE model on pages 139–141 to dispute one of your irrational beliefs.**

A – identify the *activating* event

. . . . . . . . . . . . . . . . . . . . . . . . . . . . . . . . . . . . . . . . . . . .

. . . . . . . . . . . . . . . . . . . . . . . . . . . . . . . . . . . . . . . . . . . .

. . . . . . . . . . . . . . . . . . . . . . . . . . . . . . . . . . . . . . . . . . . .

. . . . . . . . . . . . . . . . . . . . . . . . . . . . . . . . . . . . . . . . . . . .

B – note the limiting *beliefs* that accompany the event

. . . . . . . . . . . . . . . . . . . . . . . . . . . . . . . . . . . . . . . . . . . .

. . . . . . . . . . . . . . . . . . . . . . . . . . . . . . . . . . . . . . . . . . . .

. . . . . . . . . . . . . . . . . . . . . . . . . . . . . . . . . . . . . . . . . . . .

. . . . . . . . . . . . . . . . . . . . . . . . . . . . . . . . . . . . . . . . . . . .

C – what are the *consequences* of your beliefs?

. . . . . . . . . . . . . . . . . . . . . . . . . . . . . . . . . . . . . . . . . . . . . . . . . . . . . . .
. . . . . . . . . . . . . . . . . . . . . . . . . . . . . . . . . . . . . . . . . . . . . . . . . . . . . . .
. . . . . . . . . . . . . . . . . . . . . . . . . . . . . . . \. . . . . . . . . . . . . . . . . . . . . . .
. . . . . . . . . . . . . . . . . . . . . . . . . . . . . . . . . . . . . . . . . . . . . . . . . . . . . . .

D – how could you *dispute* your beliefs?

. . . . . . . . . . . . . . . . . . . . . . . . . . . . . . . . . . . . . . . . . . . . . . . . . . . . . . .
. . . . . . . . . . . . . . . . . . . . . . . . . . . . . . . . . . . . . . . . . . . . . . . . . . . . . . .
. . . . . . . . . . . . . . . . . . . . . . . . . . . . . . . . . . . . . . . . . . . . . . . . . . . . . . .
. . . . . . . . . . . . . . . . . . . . . . . . . . . . . . . . . . . . . . . . . . . . . . . . . . . . . . .

E – what is the *effect* of challenging your beliefs?

. . . . . . . . . . . . . . . . . . . . . . . . . . . . . . . . . . . . . . . . . . . . . . . . . . . . . . .
. . . . . . . . . . . . . . . . . . . . . . . . . . . . . . . . . . . . . . . . . . . . . . . . . . . . . . .
. . . . . . . . . . . . . . . . . . . . . . . . . . . . . . . . . . . . . . . . . . . . . . . . . . . . . . .
. . . . . . . . . . . . . . . . . . . . . . . . . . . . . . . . . . . . . . . . . . . . . . . . . . . . . . .

# SIXTEEN

# Reframe your negative thinking

'Today expect something good to happen to you no matter what occurred
yesterday. Let the past go. A simply abundant world awaits.'
Sarah Ban Breathnach, *Simple Abundance: A Daybook of Comfort & Joy*

Unlike most of my clients, Tom was full of anger. As soon as we
met, he unleashed all his frustrations – about his business, his
clients, his wife, his children, the government. Nothing in his
world was right.

Ironically, this same man, who had just purchased a beautiful
new home for his family and who had a substantial nest egg left over
in investments, was mostly worried about money.

Once Tom had vented his immediate frustrations, we started to
get to the heart of his concern. Beneath his furious exterior, Tom
was full of fear. His business was being impacted by the COVID-19
pandemic and there was a risk to his ongoing livelihood. Although
he had enough money to live comfortably for the rest of his life,

his perspective of reality was distorted because of the overwhelming emotion he was experiencing.

Tom had slipped into what cognitive behavioural therapists call 'automatic negative thinking'. Like most of us when we're consumed by negative thoughts, Tom's behaviour was also impacted. As well as being irritable and angry with his wife and children, Tom was impatient and intolerant with his staff. While he was experiencing an inner world of pain, Tom was also creating hostility and tension all around him.

When we experience habitual negative thoughts, we are generally very good at finding evidence that supports our negative thinking. Our minds actively search our environments for information that validates how we're thinking. Cognitive Behavioural Therapy (CBT) involves looking at the relationship between your thoughts, feelings and actions and exploring how each of these factors might be impacting your wellbeing. The theory is that when we're able to catch and correct our habitual patterns of 'faulty thinking' and we can view our circumstances more accurately, we're more likely to deal with life's challenges in positive ways.

CBT helps us to identify our false or negative thoughts and replace them with healthier, more realistic ones. It also helps us to explore how our thoughts and emotions impact our choices in life.

This popular form of therapy has been found to help create new neural pathways in the brain, literally changing the way that we think. But like any kind of change it takes practice. Most CBT programs are relatively short interventions (generally between five and 20 sessions) and the usual focus is on present-day problems that are affecting your life right now.

CBT can be used for a whole range of different issues and it's an excellent way of helping you change the way you interact with yourself. For example, if you're someone who believes you're socially awkward, when you meet someone for the first time, it's likely you'll be fixated on the thought, 'I'm terrible at meeting new people.' This makes you anxious about social events so you might avoid them altogether or feel uncomfortable when you do interact with someone new. When your thoughts are clouded with, 'I'm terrible at this. I'm not interesting. I've got nothing to talk about,' it's less likely you'll feel that you can listen intently or chat in a relaxed way. Your behaviour might even appear withdrawn or aloof, creating a perpetual cycle of thoughts, feelings and behaviours that make it difficult for you to get close to people. Eventually, you might even avoid meeting new people at all.

A CBT therapist will work with you to break this cycle, making you more aware of your inaccurate thoughts and inviting you to challenge your thinking. They'll help you to identify behaviours that are contributing to the problem so you can modify these to something more adaptive and skilful.

In a nutshell, CBT is an effective tool that encourages you to see yourself, the world and your future in a more balanced and positive way.

# Common patterns of 'faulty thinking'

1. **All or nothing / black-and-white thinking**
   You're inclined to see things in 'absolutes' and view anything short of 'perfect' as failure. Tom was convinced that his

business would fail, which meant he was also destined to personal failure. He wasn't able to see that there were options in between.

*How to challenge it*

Is there another way to think about the situation? Avoid words like 'always' or 'never' and try to view the in-between option. Remind yourself that perfection doesn't exist and despite your best efforts, you won't always have full control over every outcome.

*Reframe*

For Tom, reframing meant recognising that there were new opportunities available for his business as well as the possibility of spending more time with his family.

2. **Overgeneralisation**

If something bad happens or if you make a mistake, you expect it to happen over and over again. For example, when you try a new recipe and it fails, you tell yourself you're terrible at cooking and you won't attempt it again. We also do this in our relationships when we overgeneralise about others. You might notice that when your partner runs late or forgets something, you tell yourself that they are inconsiderate or unsupportive of you.

*How to challenge it*

Stay specific and focused on the present experience. Remember other times when you've had success with cooking other things. Recall the ways your partner is supportive of you.

*Reframe*

'That dish didn't work out but there are others that I cook really well. I want to give it another try so I'll make a few notes about what I can do differently next time.'

'My partner is a relaxed person which means they're sometimes forgetful. The upside is that they have a calming energy to be around.'

3. **Negative mental filter**

Filtering out the positive aspects of an experience and only focusing on the negatives. For example, you give a presentation and mostly it goes well but you slip up in one area. Your boss tells you the presentation was great but you can't take in the positive feedback – you're too busy ruminating over the error you made.

*How to challenge it*

Balance your thinking by also identifying the positive aspects of your experience. Try to catch yourself as you habitually turn your mind to the negatives and intentionally remind yourself of what went well.

*Reframe*

'I feel embarrassed about the mistake I made but my boss and my colleagues seemed to enjoy the presentation regardless.'

4. **Discounting the positive**

Ignoring or minimising your achievements or being dismissive of the positive things that others say about you. For example, a friend compliments you on your outfit but because you think you need to lose a few kilos, you find it difficult to take in the positive feedback.

*How to challenge it*

Remember to intentionally focus on and savour the positive things that happen to you. Allow yourself to take in a compliment and really enjoy how that feels.

*Reframe*

'This dress is flattering on me and it was really nice to be noticed.'

5.  **Jumping to conclusions / mind-reading / fortune-telling**

    Assuming that you know what others are thinking, believing that others are focused on your flaws. Feeling that someone's negative mood is your fault or responsibility. Convincing yourself that things will turn out badly. For example, not applying for an appealing new role, even though you match most of the selection criteria, because you assume that there'll be a huge number of applicants and other candidates will be better suited to the role than you.

    *How to challenge it*

    Consider all the possible scenarios, including the positive ones. Ask yourself what's possible if you continue thinking this way. How do you know this is true?

    *Reframe*

    'This is a role that I'd love and if I don't apply, I won't have a chance at all. I'm going to spend extra time on this application to give myself the best possible chance.'

6.  **Magnification or minimisation**

    Exaggerating the importance of some things and minimising the importance of others. For example, you're less extroverted than some of your friends so you tell yourself you're not good in social settings and you worry about not being a good conversationalist. You forget that when you're in company one-on-one, you feel comfortable and at ease.

*How to challenge it*

Notice your strengths and recognise when you're comparing yourself with others.

*Reframe*

'My preference is to socialise in smaller groups. I enjoy deep conversations which means I'm less interested in small talk and the light banter my friends love. This doesn't make any of us wrong – we're all different but equally valuable.'

7. **Emotional reasoning**

Assuming that your negative emotions are the complete truth and/or responsible for your behaviour. 'I feel it so this proves that it must be true.' For example, 'I feel dumb because I'm not always across the latest current affairs. I didn't complete a university degree, therefore I must be less intelligent than my friends.'

*How to challenge it*

Have you discounted positive information to the contrary? Are you 'mind-reading' what others think of your intelligence with a negative bias?

*Reframe*

'I may not know as much about politics and world events as some of my friends, but I enjoy listening to them speak about it and they seem to enjoy my questions. My interests lie in other areas and I'm intelligent when I speak about those.'

8. **Should or must statements**

A 'should' or 'must' statement infers that there are universal rules that people should follow. We sometimes use these statements to try to motivate ourselves but paradoxically, they can leave us unmotivated when we apply them to ourselves, or resentful when we apply them to others.

For example, 'I should be competent in everything I do.'

'I should exercise and eat healthy food every single day.'

*How to challenge it*

Recognise that things will rarely be *exactly* as we would like them to be. Consider how your 'should' and 'must' statements could be stated as preferences. Replace 'should' or 'must' with 'I would like to . . .', 'I want to . . .', 'I'd prefer it if . . .', 'It would be helpful if . . .' or 'I choose to . . .'

*Reframe*

'I value my health and enjoy eating wholefoods and moving my body but I also value a flexible approach. I'll eat healthily most days but I'll also thoroughly enjoy indulging in foods that I love sometimes as well as taking rest days from exercise.'

9. **Labelling or mislabelling**

Making a judgement about yourself or another person that focuses on who they are rather than what they did. For example, saying 'I am a complete idiot' rather than 'I made a clumsy remark' or 'My husband is a useless father' rather than 'My husband wasn't patient with the kids tonight.'

*How to challenge it*

Describe the circumstances objectively rather than emotionally. When you consider a behaviour to be the problem rather than the person, you'll be better able to deal with the situation calmly and effectively.

*Reframe*

'Most of my conversation is articulate and sensible but sometimes I'm less articulate.' 'My husband was tired and stressed this evening – he's generally great with the kids.'

## 10. Personalisation

Seeing yourself as the cause of everything negative including things you're not responsible for. This involves misplaced guilt and misplaced self-worth. For example, 'It's my fault that my brother has anxiety issues because I wasn't there for him enough when we were children.'

*How to challenge it*

Don't jump to conclusions or get caught in 'if only' thinking. Look for all the contributing factors and consider all the facts of the situation. Offer yourself kindness when you become aware of guilt or self-criticism.

*Reframe*

'My brother has a naturally anxious disposition and over the years, I have spent a lot of time offering strategies to help him create inner calm.'

After Tom had vented some of his frustration, we talked about how his thoughts were affecting his emotions. He was engaged in several automatic negative thoughts that were causing him a great deal of anxiety, which was presenting most often as anger. Because he was operating with a lot of adrenaline in his system, he recognised that he wasn't able to relax or enjoy other positive aspects of his life.

Tom's thought patterns were mostly black-and-white thinking and jumping to conclusions. Because he had convinced himself that his business would fail, he was consumed by thoughts about how frustrating and hopeless the situation was. He even went as far as jumping to the conclusion that he would lose his wife and children if he wasn't able to continue with the upward trajectory of financial success he had recently achieved.

## Challenge your negative thinking

- Briefly describe the situation, the automatic negative thoughts and the feelings you're experiencing.
- Describe your usual behaviour when you have these thoughts and feelings.
- Go through the ten patterns of distorted thinking listed above and notice if you're applying one or more of them. If you are, is this pattern of thinking habitual?
- Ask yourself, is this thought entirely true? Is there evidence against this thought? Is there a different way of viewing the situation? What would you say to a friend who was having this thought? How does this thought impact your behaviour?
- Can you replace an old thought with something more positive?
- Find a different way to interpret the situation and write down this new version of events.
- Notice how you feel as you read through the new version (you may want to read it several times).
- Is there an action you can take immediately or in the next few days?

# SEVENTEEN

# Choose the right mindset

*'Have patience. All things are difficult before they become easy.'*
Saadi Shirazi, 13th-century Persian poet

Our thinking styles, which most psychologists agree are generally laid down early in life, largely determine the way we approach a new challenge or any kind of change in our lives. They also determine the explanatory style we use when we find ourselves faced with adversity when we are attempting to implement change.

Amongst the many researchers on the subject of thinking styles is Carol Dweck, Professor of Psychology at Stanford University, who has spent decades researching mindset and learning about how it impacts or inhibits the choices we make in our lives.

In her book *Mindset: The New Psychology of Success*, Dweck describes two specific styles of thinking that she calls 'fixed mindset' and 'growth mindset'. She explores how these mindsets impact our motivation, our productivity and our relationships.

If you're someone with a fixed mindset, you believe your intelligence, your talents, your creative abilities and your capabilities in relationships are largely unchangeable. Dweck claims that people with this view spend a lot of time documenting their existing intelligence and talent, instead of developing it. They believe that it's *innate talent* rather than *ongoing effort* that generates success, and they prefer to hide their own deficiencies rather than owning up to or challenging them.

Thinking this way leads to less risk-taking and less of a willingness to challenge yourself or go beyond your comfort zone. Your most important objective is to avoid failing and in order to do this, you continue to operate within the boundaries of your current abilities.

Those with a growth mindset, on the other hand, are keenly interested to understand how they can develop and learn. They believe their abilities can be cultivated through dedication and hard work. They're not afraid to make mistakes and they see their basic talents and their level of intellect or creative ability as a starting point only. These people are committed to continuous learning and they see setbacks as opportunities to build resilience rather than failures.

Fixed mindset thinking suggests that you don't have the ability to tackle a certain task or solve a problem, while a growth mindset perspective is that you don't have the ability 'yet'.

I experienced the benefits of a growth mindset myself when I was in my late thirties. Since high school, I had told myself I had no creative ability, particularly in the areas of drawing and painting.

Then I heard about a book called *Drawing on the Right Side of the Brain*, written by art teacher Dr Betty Edwards in the 1970s. While teaching art, Dr Edwards was curious to understand why some of her students struggled so much to learn drawing. Working with neurobiologist Roger W. Sperry and his colleagues, she discovered that drawing is made up of five perceptual elements – and she learned that these five elements could be taught.

Dr Edwards went on to develop and teach this methodology. It made so much sense to me that I began to research courses in my local area. I found a teacher using Dr Edward's theory and as luck would have it, she was about to run a six-week beginners' drawing class.

In my first lesson, all ten participants were invited to sketch a wooden chair. I discovered pretty quickly that my class members were anything but beginners. At the end of that lesson, we were asked to display our drawings on the floor together and much to my embarrassment, my sketch was clearly the worst in the class.

The fixed mindset part of me felt reluctant to return the following week. I was frustrated at being in a class of talented artists instead of genuine beginners. As I drove home that night, I wrestled with thoughts about how unskilled I was as an artist and how I'd never be any good so it was a waste of time to continue.

After a couple of days, I managed to move past my initial embarrassment. I reminded myself that I had joined the class because I was a beginner – and because of that, I was going back the following week.

Each of those drawing classes was a challenge for me. I found it uncomfortable being the least artistic person in the room and I struggled with my lack of natural talent. But I persevered and by the end of six weeks, I had developed some basic skills in drawing.

On the final evening, when once again we displayed our works on the floor, I saw how much my drawing had improved. I realised that given my fellow students were already talented artists, I had probably gained more from those classes than anyone in the room.

I realised later that sticking with that program gave me much more than just a small amount of artistic talent. It was a reminder of how good it feels to push myself outside my comfort zone and to remember I'm resilient enough to survive an experience that is challenging.

Fixed mindset thinking often means you're unwilling to try anything new. When you're not sure you'll be able to do something well, it's easier not to try. You feel anxious about receiving negative feedback and you worry about getting it wrong.

Growth mindset, on the other hand, sees *effort* as the pathway to growth. When we adopt this mindset, we feel inspired and motivated by others' success. We view challenges as an opportunity to learn and we prioritise learning over a need for approval.

## Using growth mindset in love

We can use a growth mindset in all areas of our lives. It's helpful in the workplace, when we're learning new skills or studying, and we can also use it to change the way we interact with our loved ones.

When you enter a new relationship, for example, and you're in the early stages of infatuation, it's easy to imagine that this new partner might be 'the one' – the person you were destined to meet, the relationship that was 'meant to be'.

This early relationship phase is often coupled with biochemical changes in the brain that produce a feeling of euphoria that can be obsessive, all-consuming and idealistic. It's a phase that's known as 'limerence' and researchers have found that it rarely lasts beyond a couple of years.

With a fixed mindset, it's likely that you'll imagine that this wonderful relationship will be without challenges or conflict. You might make the assumption that if you begin to experience any difficulty, there's something fundamentally wrong with this partner. Those with a fixed mindset lose interest very quickly when conflict begins to arise. They're less inclined to take responsibility and more inclined to assign blame. They see their own abilities in a relationship as largely permanent and their partner's qualities as largely fixed. They view the relationship overall as inherently good or bad. In other words, the relationship is either *destined* to work or to fail.

This kind of 'destiny thinking' is problematic because it makes the assumption that all great relationships are built on a foundation of effortless connection. When we adopt this way of thinking, we believe that our partners will be able to anticipate our every need and we imagine that we'll always grow and develop in the same direction. We anticipate sharing the same values and interests, having similar dreams and desires, and we assume that neither of us will make any significant mistakes along the way.

Those with a growth mindset think differently. They acknowledge their own and their partner's imperfections without assigning blame. They understand that differences are sometimes problems of communication, not of inherent character, and they know that if they're able to work through conflicts and difficulties, they can build a foundation of trust. It is in this environment that genuine love will deepen and grow. Growth mindset couples are also willing to support one another's development and importantly, they're committed to remaining on the same side.

They make the assumption that:

- All human beings are inherently flawed.
- Their partner is by and large a good person.
- All relationships require work and there's no such thing as a relationship that was 'meant to be'.
- It takes effort to remain interested and engaged.
- Challenges are an opportunity to deepen the relationship.
- Blaming one another is unhelpful.
- Learning to communicate well is key.

This isn't to say that every relationship is worth fighting for, but if your rose-coloured glasses are tainting one that has promise, it might help to adopt a growth mindset.

| Fixed mindset | Growth mindset |
|---|---|
| • dislikes challenges | • welcomes challenges |
| • gives up easily | • persists in the face of adversity |
| • sees effort as pointless | • sees effort as a pathway to skill and proficiency |
| • sees criticism as negative feedback | • learns from criticism |
| • feels threatened by others | • is inspired by the success of others |
| • doesn't achieve full potential | • feels a greater sense of free will |

# Changing your mindset

At the heart of a growth mindset is a *passion for learning* rather than a *desire for approval*. Embracing this mindset means committing to continued growth, deliberate practice and a willingness to fail. Carol Dweck suggests that the willingness to challenge yourself, particularly when things aren't going well, that's at the heart of 'growth mindset'. It is this mindset that builds our resilience and helps us to thrive during the more difficult times in our lives.

If you're inclined to 'fixed mindset' thinking, try the following four steps to move into 'growth mindset' thinking.

## Step 1: Recognise and embrace both mindsets

Next time you're facing a challenging task, dealing with a setback or being confronted with criticism, tune in to your internal chatter. Learn to recognise the different voices of each mindset.

As you're about to tackle a new activity, your fixed mindset might be doubtful. 'What if I fail?' or 'It's safer not to attempt this – at least I won't make a fool of myself.' When you're facing a setback, your self-talk might be, 'Now I've embarrassed myself,' or 'I'd better make an excuse to regain my dignity.' When encountering criticism, you might find yourself feeling defensive or even angry at the other person. Your self-talk might be, 'This is not my fault.'

Your growth mindset, on the other hand, is more likely to say, 'What if I do fail at first? I can have a second (and a third) attempt.' Or, 'That was an awkward situation. Next time I'll prepare differently.' And when you encounter criticism, instead of being defensive, you might say, 'I can see where you're coming from and I'm sorry I came across that way. It wasn't my intention.'

## Step 2: Recognise that you have a choice

When you interpret a challenge, setback or criticism from a fixed mindset perspective, you make the assumption that you're lacking the skills or the talent to perform certain tasks. Or you may believe that there's something inherently wrong with you.

Choosing a growth mindset is a way of reminding yourself that you have the ability to stretch yourself and develop different skills and strategies for tackling challenging tasks.

## Step 3: Talk back to your fixed mindset with a growth mindset voice

Listen for fixed mindset thinking and challenge it by practising phrases such as, 'I can learn with a bit of effort,' or 'Most successful people have failures along the way,' or 'I can take responsibility for my part in this problem. It's an opportunity to improve things for next time.'

## Step 4: Take growth mindset action

Intentionally take on a new challenge or engage in an interest that you're not completely proficient at. When you encounter a setback or have an experience where you recognise your lack of natural ability (as I did in my drawing class), don't give up. Listen to your growth mindset and remind yourself that you're learning a new skill and it's going to take a bit of time.

As you become more comfortable embracing a growth mindset, it will become easier to move out of your comfort zone and embrace a whole range of new experiences.

# Using growth mindset when you learn a new skill

As you prepare to tackle a new challenge, remind yourself that you might not be good at your chosen skill *yet*, but that every bit of practice and every small failure is an opportunity to learn.

Try one of the following activities (or a similar example of your own) and commit to staying with it and practising on a regular basis for at least a few weeks.

- Take up a new sport that you have no experience in.
- Join a class to learn a new creative skill such as drawing, painting, ceramics or sculpture.
- Learn a new language and be open to speaking in front of your class.
- Persist with a sudoku puzzle or a crossword if you've typically found these things difficult.
- Learn to master a new software program or another piece of technology through trial and error (and be willing to fail).

# EIGHTEEN

# Boost your optimism

*'I am not what happened to me, I am what I choose to become.'*
Carl Jung

Our brains have a naturally negative bias. They evolved this way to keep us alive. If, back in primitive times, you stepped out from your hiding place with the view that the world was a safe and sunny place, it's likely you'd have missed a lurking tiger or the rival tribesman who would steal your food.

Even in the relative safety of our modern lives, we're still scanning our environments for danger. Our brains are inclined to seek out bad news, within ourselves and in the world at large, and as US psychologist Rick Hanson says, when we find that bad news, our brains cling to it tightly and we lose sight of the big picture.

We might have ten positive experiences in any given day, but if there's one that's negative, that's the one we'll focus on. Rick describes this as our brains being 'like Velcro for negative experiences and Teflon for positive ones'. Over time, this tendency can lead us into a vicious cycle of anxiety, worry and fear.

~

Camille, a confident woman in her early forties, came to see me to talk about a recent change in her thinking. With all her close friends now married and with children, she had less in common with them than ever before. While being childless had been an active choice for Camille, she had recently begun to focus on the negative aspects of her life and had started to doubt her decision not to have kids.

Camille was confused by the way she was thinking. She had never wanted children and she'd previously been content with her decision, but now that her friends' lives centred around their young families, she began to feel a distinct lack of belonging. Camille found herself overly fixated on this issue and her new preoccupation began impacting her work and her overall confidence in herself.

As Rick Hanson says, 'The brain takes the shape of whatever the mind rests upon.' In Camille's case, her habit of comparing her life to the lives of her friends was wiring her brain to believe that there was something wrong with the choice she'd made. As she slipped into the pattern of viewing herself as flawed in some way, Camille started to gather evidence to support that belief.

She became less engaged at work. Instead of leading her team with confidence, she avoided decision-making and difficult conversations. She started declining social invitations with work colleagues and her other friends and in a short space in time, she found herself caught in a pattern of negative thinking.

Camille was insightful enough to recognise that this thinking, feeling and behaviour loop would continue if she didn't do something to stop it. She and I set to work to balance the negative bias of her brain so she could start enjoying her life again.

## Balance negative thinking by savouring

As Rick says in his book *Buddha's Brain*, 'The remedy is not to suppress negative experiences; when they happen, they happen. Rather, it is to foster positive experiences – and in particular, to take them in so they become a permanent part of you.'

One way to balance negative thinking is to *actively notice and savour the positive experiences* in our days. This might include reflecting on seemingly inconsequential moments – the scent of a flower; a great cup of coffee; the smile of a passer-by; a kind word from a friend. It's also important to tune in to your own positive qualities and focus on the small wins – a conversation that went well, the completion of a task or overcoming a minor obstacle.

The way to fully savour a positive experience is to focus on it intentionally for up to 20 seconds. Bring as much of your awareness as you can to the emotions and the physical sensations that accompany the experience. Let yourself soak in *all the elements* of a single beautiful moment using every sense and feeling every positive emotion.

It's often easier to do this if you close your eyes, relax your body and imagine yourself breathing in the experience, allowing it to be absorbed by every cell in your being.

The research tells us that the longer we hold a positive thought in our awareness and the more we can fully engage with that experience, the more likely it is that we will build positive neural pathways.

# Use gratitude to balance the negative bias of the brain

Many research studies affirm that a gratitude practice helps us savour positive experiences, in turn balancing the bias of the brain, improving our health and helping us to create more connection in our relationships.

There are many different ways you can express gratitude. The key is to find a practice you enjoy and commit to that on a regular basis.

## Gratitude exercises

- Share one thing you're grateful for with your partner and/or children at the dinner table each night.
- Keep a gratitude journal and once every week, write down five things you're grateful for.
- Write a letter of gratitude to someone who has helped you in your life. Make time to meet with that person and read them your letter.
- From time to time, notice and express your gratitude to the people in your life.

# Balance pessimistic thinking

According to Martin Seligman, author of *Learned Optimism*, your 'explanatory style', or in other words, what you tell yourself when things go wrong, is impacted by three key areas – permanence, pervasiveness and personalisation.

1. **Permanence**

People who give up easily often assume that the cause of their negative experience is permanent. They believe that negative events will continue to persist and will always affect their lives. Optimists, on the other hand, believe the causes of bad events are temporary.

**Pessimists** explain good and bad events in terms of permanent causes: moods, effort, or 'always' (or in other words, 'things always go wrong for me' vs 'sometimes things go wrong but sometimes they go right'). For example, 'My boss has always hated me and our relationship will never recover.'

**Optimists** explain good and bad events in terms of transient causes: traits, abilities, 'sometimes'. For example, 'My boss is upset with me today because I made a mistake but our relationship will recover.'

2. **Pervasiveness**

Some people can easily put their troubles neatly into a box and go about the rest of their lives, even when one aspect of life is difficult. Others are inclined to catastrophising, so when one thread of their lives comes undone, the whole fabric unravels.

People who make universal explanations for their failures tend to give up on everything when they strike failure in one area. People who make specific explanations, on the other hand, may feel challenged in one part of their life but manage effectively in other areas.

**Pessimists** explain problems as universal. For example, 'James hated me. I'll never find a partner because I'm not attractive to anyone.'

**Optimists** explain problems as specific. For example, 'James hasn't asked me on another date because I wasn't what he was looking for in a partner.'

## 3. Personalisation

When bad things happen, we can blame ourselves or we can blame other circumstances. People who blame themselves when they fail often have low self-esteem as a consequence. They think they are worthless, talentless or unlovable. People who blame external events don't lose self-esteem when a negative event occurs. On the whole, they like themselves better.

**Pessimists** explain things in a personal way. For example, 'I'm hopeless with anything to do with finances.'

**Optimists** explain things in a general way. For example, 'I haven't learned about good financial management yet.'

# Realism is important too

While optimism has many positive benefits, being *overly optimistic* can be problematic too. Extreme optimists have been found to save less money, be less inclined to clear credit card debt and to overestimate how healthy and how successful they'll be.

Overoptimism has also been linked to the engagement of risk-taking behaviours such as overcommitting financially, excessive drinking and smoking and indulging in risky sexual behaviours. In my experience with clients, it can also mean denying reality or ignoring important red flags.

This was the case with Eleanor, who had been saving for six months to buy an apartment. When she came to see me, she told me about a property offer that was (in her words) 'too good to be true'.

The proposal, put to her by her financial advisor, was an off-the-plan development in one of Melbourne's most sought-after areas. The brochure was beautifully presented and the townhouse she'd earmarked to buy was stunning.

Offering financial advice is outside my realm of expertise, but I had worked with other clients in previous years who had purchased off the plan, and in both instances, those clients had lost a significant amount of money. One was unable to fund the mortgage once the property was completed because the value of the property had decreased, and the other had a range of building defects to deal with once the property had settled.

My advice to Eleanor was to seek additional information before proceeding. While her optimism and enthusiasm made her keen to leap straight in, she agreed that making such a significant financial commitment needed a good deal of research and thought.

## Teach yourself to be realistically optimistic

Next time you encounter a problem, notice how the story goes in your head. Check your 'explanatory style'. Are you saying things to yourself that sound overly negative? Are you being excessively hard on yourself?

When you notice negative thinking, do your best to change permanent explanations to impermanent ones; change pervasive explanations to specific ones, and change personal blame to a more general perspective.

If your natural style is to be overly optimistic, slow down and listen to your intuition while also looking for potential red flags.

# Believe that you are lucky too

Dr Richard Wiseman, author of *The Luck Factor*, spent eight years studying what separates lucky people from those who describe themselves as unlucky. He discovered that the most important difference is your outlook and your attitude – *lucky people think differently from others.*

Wiseman's study revealed that an individual's personality has a significant impact on how much good fortune comes into their lives. Those of us who are more anxious and inclined to negative thinking are less likely to seize opportunities as they arise. But when we believe that there is good fortune all around us, we start to see those possibilities.

In his book, Dr Wiseman outlines four essential principles to help you feel luckier.

1. **Maximise your chances to be lucky**

   Lucky people are great at creating, noticing and acting upon opportunities. They do this by maintaining and growing their personal networks, by adopting a relaxed attitude to life and by continuing to be open to new experiences.

2. **Listen to your instincts**

   Lucky people tune in to their gut instinct on a regular basis and they maximise the opportunity to be insightful by practising meditation and by reflecting on and acting on hunches.

3. **Expect to be lucky**

Lucky people believe they'll be lucky, and because of this, they also believe that the future will be full of possibility. Eventually, this expectation becomes a self-fulfilling prophecy. You're more likely to interact positively with others when you expect those interactions to be positive, and you're more likely to push through barriers and keep moving in the direction of your goals when you believe that you will ultimately succeed.

4. **Turn bad luck into good**

When something bad happens to a person who feels lucky, they turn their attention to the positives. They imagine how things could have been worse, they believe things will work out in the long run, they don't dwell on their ill fortune, they look for the 'silver lining' and they take proactive steps to improve their situation.

# NINETEEN

# Quieten your inner critic

*'Owning our story and loving ourselves through that process is the bravest thing that we will ever do.'*

Brené Brown, PhD, LMSW

In their book *Embracing Your Inner Critic*, Hal and Sidra Stone point out that each of us has many aspects of ourselves, which the authors call our sub-personalities. You might think of these as your different 'selves' or 'parts' (throughout this chapter, I'll use these terms interchangeably). Our own unique constellation of selves will vary somewhat but might, for example, include an Inner Critic, a Vulnerable Child, a People Pleaser, a Rule Maker, an Addictive Self, an Achiever, a Nurturing Parent, a Perfectionist and others. You may not be aware of all your parts at a conscious level, but behind the scenes, very often they're running your life and they can make a significant contribution to your inner and outer experience.

Dr Richard Schwartz refers to this same concept in a form of therapy called Internal Family Systems (IFS), which works at creating harmony and balance between our internal parts. Dr Schwartz suggests that while it might not always feel like it, all our parts have our best interests in mind. None are inherently 'good' or 'bad' and each has a desire to help us. They want to protect us and keep us safe in the world but sometimes one or more of these parts take their roles to an extreme. The goal of this therapy is to help you get to know your parts in order to understand the roles they play, to learn how and why they came to inhabit these roles and to become more aware of how they are currently impacting your life. Once you achieve a greater sense of awareness, you'll find it easier to create an internal sense of balance.

When you first hear about this concept, it may sound a bit strange or even 'out there'. To give you a taste of how it works, keep an open mind as you give the following exercise a try.

Next time you feel a strong emotion, try to make contact with just one of your parts. If you feel angry, for example, close your eyes and see if you can locate that anger in your body. Tune in to the sensation of anger and become curious about it. Notice if there's any judgement about feeling angry. Try to stay in touch with your Angry Part and be curious about it. Ask it some questions. *Are there other emotions there besides anger? How is this part trying to take care of you? What is it afraid of?*

As you listen deeply, it's likely you'll learn that the part is not *only* anger – it might also be fearful, lonely, anxious or sad. As you become aware of more vulnerable emotions, you may also recognise how the Angry Part is working to protect you from these vulnerable emotions.

We usually find that when we can really tune in and listen to a part, it can tell you a lot about itself and give you fascinating insights into your inner world. You may discover that this part feels much younger than you currently are. You may recognise that it has a feeling of not being understood or having been ignored or over-looked. This awareness can help you understand the origins of your Angry Part and in turn, it can help you choose how you might otherwise interact with it or the vulnerable parts it is trying to protect.

In much the same way as a real-life family operates, your internal parts function as a system within you. Each part interacts with other parts and their aim is to help you manage your inner and outer life experience. The Angry Part, for example, may not want to appear weak or vulnerable. It might use defensiveness or aggression to cover embarrassment, sadness, guilt or shame.

Most of us find that we run into trouble when we become overly identified with some parts while others are disowned or ignored.

When I first learned about IFS (which I found to be a revelation), I discovered within me a Proactive Perfectionist, an Inner Critic and an Overachiever. While these parts often took on extreme roles, I also recognised that I had disowned my Creative Self and I wasn't always in touch with the more vulnerable aspects of myself, such as my Inner Child. The proactive parts like my Perfectionist were fearful of what might occur if I let my standards relax.

Our proactive or 'protector' parts, like the ones I encountered, like to take control of our lives. These might include an Inner Controller, an Internal Judge, an Aggressive, Angry or Defensive Self, a Driven or Competitive Self. These parts are often rigid and firm and their preference is to be in command. They sometimes show up in the body as tightness or tension in the muscles or restriction in breathing.

Then there are other parts that try to protect us in different ways. A Procrastinator Self, an Addicted Self or a Lazy or Excuse-maker Self might try to numb, repress or escape from difficult feelings. They want to manage our inner hurt by keeping us from feeling our pain.

Other parts are relegated to 'exile' status. These are often our vulnerable parts, such as the Wounded or Vulnerable Child. Often, we find that our dominant parts are trying to take care of these more vulnerable parts.

Dr Schwartz suggests that these vulnerable parts may have had unmet needs when we were younger. They might have felt lonely, abandoned, unloved or worthless, and they can show up in the body as shame, guilt, depression, pain or feelings of sadness or emptiness. As well as controlling our vulnerable parts with proactive parts, we might also try to numb them with behaviours from our addictive parts.

IFS therapy helps us get to know our protector parts and understand their motivations in order for them to become less extreme. It also helps us to make contact with our vulnerable parts (who are often our 'inner children'), so that we can listen to, validate and take care of and 'unburden' them so that they are free to experience the lighter aspects of childhood such as playfulness, creativity, joy and laughter.

Once you become aware of your different parts and you're able to observe them from a place of non-judgement, you begin to see how they impact your life in helpful and unhelpful ways. From this place of awareness, you'll recognise which parts have taken on unhealthy or extreme roles and you can make a decision about what a more balanced approach might be.

You'll find you can do this most effectively when you can make contact with the part of yourself that is able to witness the internal experience. Dr Schwartz calls this 'Self' energy. I call this the *Wise Self* or my *Inner Mentor*.

## Your Wise Self

You might think of your Wise Self as your *true self* or the most grounded, calm, insightful version of you. When you're in this energy, you're likely to feel wise, confident and peaceful and it is from this place that you can begin to observe the other selves as their dynamics play out.

The Wise Self knows that all our parts are inherently useful, even the ones you disown or dislike. Each has something to teach you and once you get to know them, it's likely you'll also discover exactly how their wisdom is helpful.

Tuning in and becoming aware of the different facets of self will also help you to become more conscious of the parts that most commonly run the show. Once you have this awareness, you can learn to manage your parts internally, helping some parts to transform their roles so that you're still utilising their strengths, but operating in a more sustainable (less reactive and exhausting) way. You may also discover that your protective parts are terrified of being completely rejected and their hard work (often years of it) dismissed. There's usually a palpable sense of relief from these parts when they feel heard and appreciated and when their strengths are validated. They tend to be more open and willing to operate differently when they are actively acknowledged. It's likely you'll find that they agree to be more supportive and less critical, maybe even working alongside and supporting the Wise Self.

Ultimately, this leads to a greater sense of balance in the emotions you feel and how you behave.

## How your parts appear

You'll find you can most easily become aware of your internal parts when you engage in a regular mindfulness practice. The different aspects of self will show up in a range of ways. They might appear as mental images or inner voices, they might be felt as physical sensations, or you may experience them as emotions, behaviours or impulses.

As you begin to tune in to these internal experiences, you'll start to notice which self or part is taking control of your thoughts and emotions at any given time. With practice, you'll discover how these different parts are either helping or hindering you and eventually, you'll be able to dial up or down their intensity.

## Examples of some common parts

The Inner Critic is a harsh judge of everything you do.

**Common messages:**
*I'm too sensitive / boring / selfish / inconsiderate / unlovable
/ lazy.*
*I'm too tall / short / heavy / thin / unattractive.*
*I'm not smart / funny / outgoing enough.*
*I'm such an idiot, I shouldn't have said that stupid thing.*
*I'm so lazy, I should have exercised today.*

The Vulnerable Child feels afraid, sad, anxious and alone.

**Common messages:**

*No one is there to support me.*

*Things are difficult for me.*

*I'm not strong enough.*

*I can't handle things on my own.*

*I'm unlovable and I'll always be alone.*

The People Pleaser puts everyone else first.

**Common messages:**

*I must be liked by everyone.*

*I must always be 'nice'.*

*It's selfish to put my needs first.*

*I need to give more to others.*

The Perfectionist is closely linked to the Inner Critic.

**Common messages:**

*I must do everything perfectly all the time.*

*I must excel in all areas of my life.*

*I must look attractive at all times.*

*I must only have positive thoughts.*

The Wise Self is the most grounded, open, non-judgemental aspect of yourself.

**Common messages:**

*I know I'm not perfect but I'm good enough.*

*It's helpful for me to take care of my own needs too.*

*It's okay to make mistakes sometimes, this is how I learn.*

*I'm learning to be more grounded, confident and calm.*

# Who are your parts?

You may find it easiest at first to identify parts that are in opposition to one another. For example, your People Pleaser will be kind and generous to others but it may find it hard to set boundaries or take care of your own needs. When you're overidentified with this part, it's unlikely you'll engage your Assertive Self, for fear of offending or upsetting someone.

Your Procrastinator is often in conflict with your Overachiever. The Procrastinator can find a multitude of ways to distract you from your tasks while the Overachiever wants to push you to keep working.

When you become aware of this internal conflict, you might also discover that your Wise Self (or Inner Mentor) encourages the People Pleaser to step back and let the Assertive Self have a say. The Wise Self might encourage the Overachiever to ease off a bit and make time for rest so you don't run yourself into the ground.

It's helpful to acknowledge that the Wise Self may need some help or practice in developing their role. To help strengthen this part, consider what you'd say to a good friend who was going through a similar situation or what one of your supportive mentors would advise you to do.

Grab your journal or a blank sheet of paper and make a note of the most dominant selves you're aware of, including those that are in opposition to one another. For example, you might have an Overachiever while at the same time, a Procrastinator or even just a Relaxed Self.

Come up with your own names for each of your parts and reflect on how they help or hinder you in life. You may find it helpful to use a sense of humour as you complete this exercise because it really can feel a little unusual at first!

. . . . . . . . . . . . . . . . . . . . . . . . . . . . . . . . . . . . . . . . . . . . . . . .

. . . . . . . . . . . . . . . . . . . . . . . . . . . . . . . . . . . . . . . . . . . . . . . .

. . . . . . . . . . . . . . . . . . . . . . . . . . . . . . . . . . . . . . . . . . . . . . . .

. . . . . . . . . . . . . . . . . . . . . . . . . . . . . . . . . . . . . . . . . . . . . . . .

. . . . . . . . . . . . . . . . . . . . . . . . . . . . . . . . . . . . . . . . . . . . . . . .

. . . . . . . . . . . . . . . . . . . . . . . . . . . . . . . . . . . . . . . . . . . . . . . .

. . . . . . . . . . . . . . . . . . . . . . . . . . . . . . . . . . . . . . . . . . . . . . . .

. . . . . . . . . . . . . . . . . . . . . . . . . . . . . . . . . . . . . . . . . . . . . . . .

. . . . . . . . . . . . . . . . . . . . . . . . . . . . . . . . . . . . . . . . . . . . . . . .

# Working with your different parts

Read through the following instructions in full before reflecting on your answers and have your notebook and a pen handy to jot down any insights you have.

Begin by focusing on a single issue you'd like to address in your life. For example, you may feel that you'd like to become more assertive.

Close your eyes and think about the emotions that accompany the idea of addressing this issue, such as fear of offending or hurting someone if you say 'no', for example.

As you focus on these emotions, think about the *part of your personality* that drives these emotions. In this case, it might be your People Pleaser.

Now see if you can connect with your Wise Self. Remember, this is the part of you that is non-judgemental, open, accepting and curious. With your awareness on the Wise Self, ask the other part a few questions, which might feel a little odd at first. *How is it trying to help you? Is there something it wants you to know?*

Just allow any answers to arise in their own time. For example, your People Pleaser might tell you it wants you to be considerate of others and unselfish and kind. It might tell you that it's worried about upsetting someone, causing conflict or even getting into trouble.

Next, with the help of the Wise Self, see if you can imagine what a more balanced approach might be. Is there another part that could help you create change? For example, your Assertive Self (which might be a kind and generous Assertive Self) might be able to step in and offer a few pre-prepared phrases that will help you when your People Pleaser finds it hard to set boundaries, such as, *'Thanks for the invitation to help. I'm at capacity at the moment. I will let you know if that changes.'*

If you find it difficult to access your different parts, you may find it helpful to spend some time meditating or journalling each day over the coming week to try connecting with your inner selves.

Try to give each of your parts some space – free from interruption from other parts – to be listened to, especially when exploring parts in opposition with each other. You might want to let the parts know that each will have their turn to be heard. If you find a part dominating, ask if they could step back and just listen when another part is offering its perspective.

Over time and with practice, you'll become more adept at catching your parts at play and you may find, that like most people, you have the ability to resolve many of your own problems by accessing your own internal wisdom.

## Your Inner Critic

Much of our inner conflict occurs subconsciously. We may not realise it, but we're often measuring ourselves against who we think we should be according to our parents, friends, society and our own high expectations of ourselves. The internal voice that criticises you mercilessly is what Hal and Sidra Stone called the Inner Critic.

As the Stones point out, the original role of the Inner Critic was positive – its aim was to protect you from pain and shame by criticising you before anyone else could. The problem is that this voice can become *incessantly* critical. In an attempt to make sure you are always perceived as attractive, likeable, careful and successful, it expends a great deal of energy worrying about what others think and it doesn't know when to let up.

My client Olivia had a strong Inner Critic. Since her early teens, she'd had an uncomfortable relationship with her body and a difficult relationship with food. Although she was within a reasonable weight range, she wasn't stick-thin like a few of her friends. In an ongoing battle that had lasted two decades, Olivia had created a long list of 'shoulds' about her appearance and how she must take care of her physical wellbeing.

She went through cycles of gruelling exercise and restricting food followed by months of no exercise and unhealthy eating. In her 'good' months, she would drop several kilos and feel great about her appearance, and in her 'bad' months, she felt flawed and ashamed of her body.

Olivia's Inner Critic was fixated on the idea that in order to be attractive and lovable, she *must* look a certain way, and an important aspect of that was her weight.

As Olivia began working on her body image concerns, she started to recognise an internal argument between her Inner Critic and a kinder, more compassionate part that she called her Inner Mentor (which was Olivia's name for her Wise Self). She also became aware that her Vulnerable Child part wanted to be able to eat normally and be accepted and loved for who she is, regardless of her physical appearance.

Accessing and strengthening her Inner Mentor helped the Inner Critic, in time, relax and trust that she knew how to take better care of the Vulnerable Child part. With the help of an IFS therapist, Olivia was able to make peace with her body, create a happier relationship with food and find pleasure through a few forms of exercise she loved.

## Get to know your Inner Critic

Spend some time journalling on the origins of your Inner Critic. When did you notice it first? What brought it into being? Does it sound like the voice of a family member (a parent, sibling or grandparent), a teacher or a friend you had at school?

. . . . . . . . . . . . . . . . . . . . . . . . . . . . . . . . . . . . . . . . . . . . .

. . . . . . . . . . . . . . . . . . . . . . . . . . . . . . . . . . . . . . . . . . . . .

. . . . . . . . . . . . . . . . . . . . . . . . . . . . . . . . . . . . . . . . . . . . .

. . . . . . . . . . . . . . . . . . . . . . . . . . . . . . . . . . . . . . . . . . . . .

. . . . . . . . . . . . . . . . . . . . . . . . . . . . . . . . . . . . . . . . . . . . .

**What does your Inner Critic say?**

. . . . . . . . . . . . . . . . . . . . . . . . . . . . . . . . . . . . . . . . . . . . . . . .
. . . . . . . . . . . . . . . . . . . . . . . . . . . . . . . . . . . . . . . . . . . . . . . .
. . . . . . . . . . . . . . . . . . . . . . . . . . . . . . . . . . . . . . . . . . . . . . . .

# Get to know your Wise Self

Now see if you can make contact with your Wise Self. Think back to a time in your life when you felt grounded, confident and calm. It may have been at work when you were dealing with a challenge, with family or a friend when you were being supportive, or maybe in a crisis situation where you found yourself able to be centred and clear-thinking. Describe the scenario and the qualities and characteristics of your Wise Self.

. . . . . . . . . . . . . . . . . . . . . . . . . . . . . . . . . . . . . . . . . . . . . . . .
. . . . . . . . . . . . . . . . . . . . . . . . . . . . . . . . . . . . . . . . . . . . . . . .
. . . . . . . . . . . . . . . . . . . . . . . . . . . . . . . . . . . . . . . . . . . . . . . .
. . . . . . . . . . . . . . . . . . . . . . . . . . . . . . . . . . . . . . . . . . . . . . . .

**What advice would your Wise Self offer you?**

Reflecting back on the issue you used in the earlier exercise, consider the advice your Wise Self would offer you.

. . . . . . . . . . . . . . . . . . . . . . . . . . . . . . . . . . . . . . . . . . . . . . . .
. . . . . . . . . . . . . . . . . . . . . . . . . . . . . . . . . . . . . . . . . . . . . . . .
. . . . . . . . . . . . . . . . . . . . . . . . . . . . . . . . . . . . . . . . . . . . . . . .
. . . . . . . . . . . . . . . . . . . . . . . . . . . . . . . . . . . . . . . . . . . . . . . .
. . . . . . . . . . . . . . . . . . . . . . . . . . . . . . . . . . . . . . . . . . . . . . . .
. . . . . . . . . . . . . . . . . . . . . . . . . . . . . . . . . . . . . . . . . . . . . . . .
. . . . . . . . . . . . . . . . . . . . . . . . . . . . . . . . . . . . . . . . . . . . . . . .

# TWENTY

# Overcome imposter syndrome

*'To be yourself in a world that is constantly trying to make you something else is the greatest accomplishment.'*

Ralph Waldo Emerson

Rosa was quiet by nature, hardworking and intelligent. She held a senior position in a communications company and performed her role well. She was on good terms with her manager and enjoyed her work for the most part, but she spent a lot of time comparing herself unfavourably to her more outgoing, outspoken colleagues. She worried that one day she'd be tapped on the shoulder and told she'd been 'found out'.

If you've ever minimised your accomplishments and considered them to have been the result of luck rather than competence, or if you've had to fight the persistent fear that you're a fraud who's going to be uncovered at any second, then, like Rosa, you've experienced imposter syndrome.

# What's your imposter style?

Dr Valerie Young, internationally-known expert on imposter syndrome and author of award-winning book *The Secret Thoughts of Successful Women: Why Capable People Suffer from the Impostor Syndrome and How to Thrive in Spite of It* has spent decades studying these feelings. She notes that in high achievers, imposter syndrome is the tendency we have to 'discount or diminish obvious evidence of our abilities'. Dr Young has categorised five different types of people who suffer from imposter syndrome.

The first is the Perfectionist, whose focus is on *how* something is done. Perfectionists set unrealistic standards for how something should turn out, and they believe failing to meet those standards is confirmation that they don't belong.

The second type, the Expert, is like the Perfectionist, but their main concern is around *what* they know. They expect themselves to know 'everything' about the arena in which they are operating. Anything that exposes that they don't know everything leads to a sense of failure and shame.

The Soloist is the third type. They are focused on the *who*. In order to feel worthy of an achievement or accolade, they need to have done it all by themselves. They believe if they require help, then they're not deserving.

The fourth type in Young's categorisations is the Natural Genius, who cares deeply about *how* and *when* accomplishments occur. If it takes more than one attempt for them to master a skill, or deliver an outcome, they feel a deep sense of failure and shame.

And then there is the Superwoman/Superman/Super Student.

These people measure their competence on *how many* roles they can excel at. If they are shining at work but falling short as a parent, they feel like a fraud. These people feel they should be exceptional at every role in their life all at the same time.

It's been estimated that over 70 per cent of people will experience imposter syndrome at some time in their lives and the irony is that people who feel like imposters are usually anything but. They're more often than not the highest achievers.

When she was the guest of honour at the 2007 Women in Entertainment Power 100 event, actress Jodie Foster admitted, 'I always feel like something of an imposter. I don't know what I'm doing.'

In an interview with the *New York Times*, Howard Schultz (chairman, president and CEO of Starbucks) said, 'Very few people, whether you've been in that job before or not, get into the seat and believe today that they are now qualified to be the CEO. They're not going to tell you that, but it's true.'

## Stop thinking like an imposter

In order to overcome imposter syndrome, you need to *stop thinking like an imposter*. Start to recognise the thoughts that trigger you specifically. This will help you understand which of the five categories you best fit into (and you may fit more than one), making it easier to catch imposter syndrome when it rears its head. Once you have this awareness, try to set the bar of 'competence' at a more realistic level and reframe your self-critical thoughts. Over time, you'll find that thinking differently will help you choose behaviours that are more likely to boost your confidence.

- Read the mindset chapter (page 155) again and remind yourself that non-imposters seek constant improvement, not because they see themselves as flawed but because they see the benefits of continued learning.
- Start to view constructive criticism as an opportunity to improve, rather than proof of your defectiveness.
- Keep working on building your relationship with your Inner Mentor and quietening your Inner Critic.
- Remind yourself that mastering a new skill takes time. Not being good at something initially doesn't mean you're inept – it simply means you need more practice.
- Keep in mind that no matter how good you are, no one does everything perfectly all the time. It's okay to have setbacks and to make mistakes. It's how you respond to them that counts.
- Remember that it's okay to not know the answer.
- Not feeling confident about a certain task doesn't mean you lack confidence overall. It only means you're not confident in this one area (and maybe you don't need to be).
- When you do have a setback, make a mistake or experience embarrassment, use mindfulness and self-compassion as you allow for your disappointment.

Given that imposter syndrome triggers feelings of shame, it's also often shrouded in secrecy. Find a support person to help you defuse feelings of shame and to remind you that you're not alone, but as Dr Young says, don't get caught thinking that talking about imposter syndrome will resolve it. Her research has found that discussing it and getting caught in a pattern of ruminating on how much you're an imposter without acting to change your thoughts and behaviours, can continue to keep you stuck.

## Fake it until you make it

Fear and excitement create the same feelings in the body – the difference in how you deal with those feelings is what you tell yourself about them. This was one of the most helpful lessons for me in my early days of public speaking. I had the idea that I could only present to a group once I'd overcome my nerves, yet despite months of practice at Toastmasters and workshops on public speaking, I still walked onto every stage feeling anxious.

Only after spending a weekend with speaking coach Robert Rabbin, who later became a dear friend before passing away in 2017, did I understand that fear could be part of the journey. 'What does it matter if you're afraid?' Robert asked me. 'Get up there and speak anyway. Stop thinking about yourself and focus on what you have to share.'

Robert reminded me that no matter how competent I became in speaking or how many years I practised, there would still be days when I messed up my words or lost my place, in the same way that I occasionally lost my focus in a conversation with a friend. He made me recognise how normal it was to be flawed. 'Just walk onto that stage and tell yourself you're there to share something you care about,' he told me. 'And don't be so caught up in your ego that you think you need to be perfect.'

With these thoughts inside my head, and with Robert's belief in me, I found that I could make room for my fear and even enjoy myself. As he had role-modelled so often, I also took myself a lot less seriously.

Create a picture in your mind of the confident version of yourself tackling one of the tasks you find challenging. Remember that even with your inner anxieties, your outer demeanour can make all the difference.

Expect to feel nervous but don't allow those nerves to define you. Remind yourself that they're the same nerves that Jodie Foster, Meryl Streep, Sheryl Sandberg, Tom Hanks, Michelle Obama, Harold Schwartz, Maya Angelou and a host of other brilliant people have described feeling. You're certainly not on your own.

## Choose a challenge for yourself

In the coming days, move out of your comfort zone in one of the following ways (or come up with a few ideas of your own).

- Speak up in a meeting.
- Offer to present to your team.
- Write an opinion piece and send it off to your local newspaper.
- Ask for a promotion or a pay rise.
- Open up an honest conversation with someone you love.

## Changing the rules in your mind

Dr Young suggests we all have rules (conscious or not) in our heads about what defines 'competent' in our particular arena. We tell ourselves, 'If I were really intelligent, capable, competent . . .'

- I would know what to say on the spot.
- I'd have all the right answers.
- I'd be confident to speak up in meetings.
- I would be articulate and wise.
- I would appear more confident.

I invited Rosa to give this exercise a try. She made a list of all the different ways she was criticising herself and she could see how often she was caught in the belief that 'she must be perfect and competent at all times'.

Rosa identified her style as Perfectionistic and she recognised that her thinking was very unrealistic. We spoke about her relationship with failure. Rather than seeing it as confirmation that she was a fraud, we worked on seeing failure as a chance to boost her expertise and competence.

## What are you telling yourself?

Using the following phrase as a prompt, write down all the different ways you are self-critical.

For example: *If I were really intelligent, capable, competent . . .*

- I'd always know the right answer.
- I would never make a mistake.
- I would be more successful.
- People would listen to me more in meetings.
- I'd be more popular.

. . . . . . . . . . . . . . . . . . . . . . . . . . . . . . . . . . . . . . . . . . . . . . . . .

. . . . . . . . . . . . . . . . . . . . . . . . . . . . . . . . . . . . . . . . . . . . . . . . .

. . . . . . . . . . . . . . . . . . . . . . . . . . . . . . . . . . . . . . . . . . . . . . . . .

. . . . . . . . . . . . . . . . . . . . . . . . . . . . . . . . . . . . . . . . . . . . . . . . .

. . . . . . . . . . . . . . . . . . . . . . . . . . . . . . . . . . . . . . . . . . . . . . . . .

. . . . . . . . . . . . . . . . . . . . . . . . . . . . . . . . . . . . . . . . . . . . . . . . .

**What would a non-imposter think?**

For example: *Given I'm intelligent, capable, competent and imperfect . . .*

- I know there'll be times when I don't have all the answers.
- Sometimes I'll get it wrong and that's okay.
- I'm progressing at a reasonable pace.
- I'm working on becoming a more confident presenter.
- I accept that not everyone will like me.

........................................................

........................................................

........................................................

........................................................

........................................................

........................................................

# TWENTY-ONE

# Create possibility

*'I will love the light for it shows me the way, yet I will endure the darkness for it shows me the stars.'*

Og Mandino

When Yael was a child, she spent a lot of time painting, drawing, crafting, making and photographing. There was nothing she loved more than a new set of watercolour paints or being given a canvas as a gift. But at a certain point in her teens she stopped creating. The influence of her peer group and the pursuit of good marks at school took priority over everything else.

Yael studied finance at university and went on to become an accountant. While there were aspects she enjoyed about managing people's finances, she found herself longing for a career that was more creative. Her secret dream was to one day make her living as an artist, but it seemed like a long way from how she spent her days now. Most of the artists Yael followed on Instagram had been drawing and painting for years, so she felt she'd never catch up.

I urged her to adopt the mindset of 'creating possibility'.

It's a mindset that involves taking personal responsibility for effecting change rather waiting for an opportunity to magically appear. It involves letting yourself be seen and stepping out of your comfort zone as well as putting aside the excuses and limiting realities you've created for yourself.

Rosamund and Benjamin Zander are the authors of *The Art of Possibility: Transforming Personal and Professional Life*. In their book they propose the idea that 'all reality is invented', by which they mean that we humans take inputs (information, occurrences) from our environment and use those inputs to create constructs. These constructs take the form of assumptions that are characterised by phrases such as:

*I could never . . .*

*I shouldn't . . .*

*I can only . . .*

These assumptions grow into narratives that travel with us through our lives. Yael's narrative was that she'd missed the boat with regard to having a creative career. She felt that in choosing the accounting career path, she'd locked the doors on a creative path forever.

The assumptions you make shape your reality. But in the same way we can create limiting assumptions, so too can we create assumptions that free us from limitations.

As the Zanders note in *The Art of Possibility*:

*. . . many of the circumstances that seem to block us in our*
*daily lives may only appear to do so based on a framework*
*of assumptions we carry with us. Draw a different frame*
*around the same set of circumstances and new pathways come*
*into view.*

The path to possibility is paved by your own personal perspective. If you impose limitations on yourself, this is all you'll see. If you remove those self-imposed limitations, the path clears and becomes easier to traverse.

## Clear the path to possibility

Sometimes by the time we reach adulthood, we've received the message loud and clear that there's little point in daring to dream because many of our dreams are unrealistic.

An easy way to identify dreams that are lying latent beneath the surface is to take note of the people you follow on social media and the things you see them doing that create in you a pang of envy or yearning.

Yael followed many artists on Instagram and she found herself feeling envious when she saw one of those artists opening an exhibition. A big part of her artist dream was to exhibit her work.

Not every hankering or feeling of envy is an indication that something is a 'real' dream of yours, but if you find yourself returning to the same themes again and again over a long period of time, it's worth taking note.

In order to clear a path to possibility, you first need to identify the limitations you've placed on yourself achieving your closely held dreams.

Yael's list of self-imposed limitations was lengthy:

- It's been so long since I've done any sketching, I'm not even sure I know how anymore.
- The gap between my talent and the people I admire is huge. I would feel like an imposter even calling myself an artist.

- As an artist, I couldn't replicate the income I make as an accountant.
- There's not enough space in my apartment to set up a studio.
- There are no artists in my family, and my parents wouldn't be overly supportive of me making such a huge career pivot.
- My friends would think I was crazy.

While barriers sometimes seem insurmountable, they can always be challenged. Here's how Yael reframed hers:

- It's been a long time since I've sketched but it's not too late to pick up my pencils. I'm going to start today.
- It's true that the people I admire are producing work well beyond what I can produce now, and might ever be able to produce, but I don't need to measure myself by their standards or even be the best artist to enjoy the process of making art.
- Maybe art doesn't have to replace my accountant income. I can make a few lifestyle choices that reduce my cost of living and continue to work part-time as an accountant.
- I don't need a studio in order to be able to create art.
- While the support of my family and friends would always make things easier, I have enough internal drive to make this happen. And who knows, maybe my family will come around once they see how important this is to me.

Challenging our beliefs and assumptions might initially feel hard, but it's also incredibly freeing to see how the barriers you thought were insurmountable aren't actually as intimidating as they first seemed.

Once you experience the boost of energy that comes from breaking down those barriers, it can be very tempting to go all in and make huge changes in your life all at once in the pursuit of your dream. While the 'go big' approach works for a rare few, most people's success is years in the making. It's generally the result of mapping out a path of small stepping stones, overcoming the setbacks you encounter along the way and staying committed to your dream.

Yael set about doing just that. She carried a sketchbook and pencils at all times and when she found herself at a cafe, or on a train commuting, instead of scrolling through her phone, she started sketching.

After a few months, she had built up enough confidence to start sharing some of her sketches on Instagram. This gave her the chance to 'practise in public'. She played with different styles – pen drawings, pencil sketches, small watercolour paintings – and paid attention to what people responded to most strongly.

She joined an art class and spent a year filling her social media feed with little pieces of art. She caught the attention of a working artist who lived nearby, and six months later she invited Yael to exhibit her work in a group exhibition she was curating. Yael was ecstatic. In less than two years, she'd gone from 'I've missed the boat on ever becoming an artist' to exhibiting her work alongside other artists she greatly admired. And she got there while continuing to work full-time as an accountant and making art in her tiny apartment.

Yael found that having a regular source of income from her day job gave her the freedom to create art in the evenings and on the weekends without the pressure of needing to make money from that art.

You may find, like Yael did, that your future dreams can sit alongside your current circumstances once you challenge the assumptions and beliefs you have about those circumstances.

## Exercises to help create possibility
**What's your secret dream?**

. . . . . . . . . . . . . . . . . . . . . . . . . . . . . . . . . . . . . . . . . . . .

. . . . . . . . . . . . . . . . . . . . . . . . . . . . . . . . . . . . . . . . . . . .

. . . . . . . . . . . . . . . . . . . . . . . . . . . . . . . . . . . . . . . . . . . .

**What are your limiting assumptions?**

. . . . . . . . . . . . . . . . . . . . . . . . . . . . . . . . . . . . . . . . . . . .

. . . . . . . . . . . . . . . . . . . . . . . . . . . . . . . . . . . . . . . . . . . .

. . . . . . . . . . . . . . . . . . . . . . . . . . . . . . . . . . . . . . . . . . . .

**How can you create possibility by reframing the limiting beliefs?**

. . . . . . . . . . . . . . . . . . . . . . . . . . . . . . . . . . . . . . . . . . . .

. . . . . . . . . . . . . . . . . . . . . . . . . . . . . . . . . . . . . . . . . . . .

. . . . . . . . . . . . . . . . . . . . . . . . . . . . . . . . . . . . . . . . . . . .

**List three 'stepping stone' actions you can take.**

1 . . . . . . . . . . . . . . . . . . . . . . . . . . . . . . . . . . . . . . . . . . .

2 . . . . . . . . . . . . . . . . . . . . . . . . . . . . . . . . . . . . . . . . . . .

3 . . . . . . . . . . . . . . . . . . . . . . . . . . . . . . . . . . . . . . . . . . .

# TWENTY-TWO

# Make it a habit

*'I was always looking outside myself for strength and confidence, but it comes from within. It is there all the time.'*

Anna Freud

My friend Rachel appears to be incredibly disciplined. She exercises every day and if she makes a promise, she always follows through. She eats well because she finds it easier to *maintain* a healthy weight than to be gaining weight she then needs to lose.

Yet, whenever someone refers to her as 'disciplined', Rachel thinks that the opposite is true. She knows that while her behaviour might appear disciplined, she's not naturally wired that way.

In her teenage years, Rachel was a classic procrastinator. She felt as though she was always lurching from one disaster to another. Assignments were routinely finished in the school library during the lunch break before they were due. She'd often find herself racing through the house looking for something crucial two minutes before she was meant to be jumping on the school bus, and she was always letting friends down because she couldn't remember what she'd committed to.

Rachel credits good habits for transforming her from someone who frequently double-booked herself to someone who now feels that she has her life in order.

In his *New York Times* bestselling book *Atomic Habits*, James Clear suggests: 'The ultimate purpose of habits is to solve the problems of life with as little energy and effort as possible.'

This is exactly what Rachel has done. She assessed the problems she was having in life (always putting herself under pressure by leaving things until the last minute and being seen as unreliable by her friends and family) and created a suite of habits that addressed those problems.

Often when we decide we want to create new habits, we set goals that are too lofty or too rigid. At the first sign of failure or non-compliance, we berate ourselves for not being disciplined or having enough self-control.

In *Atomic Habits*, Clear notes that self-control is a short-term strategy, not a long-term one, and that people who appear to have excellent self-control are not necessarily more disciplined than others, they simply spend less time in tempting situations.

A major key is to set up your environment to facilitate success.

Take a moment now to step through your day and note all the behaviours you indulge in that are fairly unthinking. They might include:

- Reaching for your phone as soon as you wake up.
- Making a coffee when you first enter your kitchen in the morning.
- Looking at social media while you drink your coffee.
- Getting a pastry from the cafe next to work at morning-tea time.

- Eating lunch at your desk.
- Taking your dog for a walk when you get home from work.
- Pouring a glass of wine while you cook dinner.
- Eating the leftovers on your kids' plates.

Once you've made your list, write next to the behaviour whether it's 'favourable', 'unfavourable' or 'neutral'. You might be dismayed to find that, of the things you do unthinkingly, more are 'unfavourable' habits than neutral or positive.

This is because the reward of an unfavourable habit is often experienced in the moment. The reward of eating a chocolate biscuit, for example, is experienced while you eat it. This strong feedback loop means it's very easy to develop the habit of reaching for one every time you open the pantry.

On the flip side, the reward for a good habit, like going for a walk every day, is seldom experienced in the moment, or even immediately after. You might feel good after going for a walk, but not *so* good that the behaviour becomes automatic. The real rewards of a daily walking habit tend to be experienced after sticking to that habit for several weeks. If you find it frustrating that the act of getting dressed in exercise gear and heading out the door never becomes automatic, it's important to understand this: *when you're trying to create a good habit, the goal isn't to make it effortless and automatic. The goal is to reduce the effort involved in executing the desired behaviour.*

B. J. Fogg, the director of the Stanford University Behaviour Design Lab, has been researching behaviour for over 20 years and developed the Tiny Habits program in 2011. Fogg contends that only three things lead to behaviour change in the long term:

1. Have an epiphany
2. Change your environment
3. Take baby steps

Since having an epiphany is hard to engineer in humans, he built his Tiny Habits program around the other two things: changing your environment and taking baby steps.

Changing your environment is a key factor in reducing the effort required to perform a task. This in turn reduces the need to call on your finite resources of self-control and discipline.

The simple act of laying out your exercise clothes the night before boosts your chances of going for a walk in the morning. Those who work from home know that doing their household chores before sitting down to work will increase their ability to be productive (because they've removed a common distraction). People who want to eat more fruit know that having a visible fruit bowl on the kitchen counter makes them more likely to eat the fruit than if they have to head to the shops to buy it.

The same principle works in reverse for when you want to break a bad habit. You can set up your environment to make a bad habit harder to do.

If you find yourself going to the fridge and grabbing a snack every time you're bored, you might try making sure there are no snacks in the fridge. If your phone is a constant temptation when you're trying to work, put it out of the room or in flight mode. If your nightly Netflix habit is affecting your ability to get enough sleep, set your internet modem to switch off at a certain time each night.

The other key principle of Fogg's Tiny Habits program is the directive to take very small steps. He gives the example of creating a daily flossing habit by setting the bar at flossing one single tooth each day. In other words, make the new habit so small, it would almost be ridiculous not to do it. And he advocates *keeping* the bar at that level. If you always end up flossing more than one tooth each day, great. But don't set the standard any higher than that one tooth.

If you want to apply this principle to creating a daily walking habit, you could set the bar at walking for just a few minutes each day. By keeping the standard low and easy to execute, you increase the chances of turning that activity into a habit.

Fogg also believes that it's important to celebrate when you've completed the activity you set out to do. He says:

*When you do a behavior and feel a positive emotion about it, your brain pays attention. It essentially thinks, 'Wow, that felt good. I want to do that behavior again!'*

Celebrating could be as simple as saying 'well done' to yourself when you walk through the door at the end of your walk but it could equally mean rewarding yourself with a bunch of flowers or a massage at the end of the week.

Another great way to form good new habits is called habit stacking. This is where you attach a new habit to an existing one. The existing habit then acts as an effective trigger for the new one.

The 'formula' for habit stacking is: *After/before [CURRENT HABIT], I will [NEW HABIT]*.

If you were to apply this technique to the daily walking habit, you might attach the action of getting changed into your exercise gear to another morning habit. For example, *After I have my morning cup of coffee, I will put on my exercise gear.*

If you've already laid out your outfit the night before (setting up your environment to facilitate success), it should be easy to put on those clothes straight after your morning coffee.

From there, the tiny action of walking for a couple of minutes will seem so easy, it would be silly not to do it. Once you're out the door and walking, chances are you'll walk for longer than that.

Once you've finished your walk, celebrating will create a positive feedback loop that makes it easier to repeat the whole thing again the next morning.

Once you've gone through the process a few times, you'll note how little you've had to call on self-control or discipline to get out for your daily walk because all the heavy lifting is being done by the system you've created: a system that becomes a habit after enough repetition and reinforcement.

An additional focus in effective habit formation is understanding how your new habits fit with your identity. Rachel used to be someone who was unreliable and always leaving things to the last second, and now she sees herself as someone who is dependable, healthy and has her life in good order.

You might currently think of yourself as 'not an exerciser' and this might lead to you doing things that affect your ability to get out the door each morning for a walk. Maybe you stay up late watching Netflix or you wait until just before your scheduled walk time to try and locate your exercise gear.

In *Atomic Habits* James Clear suggests a simple two-step process to counter this self-sabotage:

1. Decide the type of person you want to be.
2. Prove it to yourself with small wins.

Tell yourself, 'I'm the kind of person who exercises every day' and then prove it to yourself by heading out the door each morning and walking for at least a couple of minutes. Each time you perform that activity, you are providing evidence to yourself that you're the kind of person who exercises every day.

Eventually, this will become part of your identity and you won't need to prove it to yourself anymore and an added bonus is this small shift in the way you see yourself will likely lead to other positive changes as well.

## What's one new habit you'll commit to this week?

Resist the urge to change everything all at once and instead, choose one habit that will allow you to take a step towards that identity.

**What's your new habit?**

. . . . . . . . . . . . . . . . . . . . . . . . . . . . . . . . . . . . . . . . . . . . . . . . . .

. . . . . . . . . . . . . . . . . . . . . . . . . . . . . . . . . . . . . . . . . . . . . . . . . .

. . . . . . . . . . . . . . . . . . . . . . . . . . . . . . . . . . . . . . . . . . . . . . . . . .

**How will you set up your environment in a way that promotes that habit?**

. . . . . . . . . . . . . . . . . . . . . . . . . . . . . . . . . . . . . . . . . . . . . . . . . .

. . . . . . . . . . . . . . . . . . . . . . . . . . . . . . . . . . . . . . . . . . . . . . . . . .

. . . . . . . . . . . . . . . . . . . . . . . . . . . . . . . . . . . . . . . . . . . . . . . . . .

**Which existing habit can you stack this habit onto?**

. . . . . . . . . . . . . . . . . . . . . . . . . . . . . . . . . . . . . . . . . . . . . . . . . .

. . . . . . . . . . . . . . . . . . . . . . . . . . . . . . . . . . . . . . . . . . . . . . . . . .

. . . . . . . . . . . . . . . . . . . . . . . . . . . . . . . . . . . . . . . . . . . . . . . . . .

**What kind of person do you want to be?**

. . . . . . . . . . . . . . . . . . . . . . . . . . . . . . . . . . . . . . . . . . . .

. . . . . . . . . . . . . . . . . . . . . . . . . . . . . . . . . . . . . . . . . . . .

. . . . . . . . . . . . . . . . . . . . . . . . . . . . . . . . . . . . . . . . . . . .

. . . . . . . . . . . . . . . . . . . . . . . . . . . . . . . . . . . . . . . . . . . .

. . . . . . . . . . . . . . . . . . . . . . . . . . . . . . . . . . . . . . . . . . . .

. . . . . . . . . . . . . . . . . . . . . . . . . . . . . . . . . . . . . . . . . . . .

. . . . . . . . . . . . . . . . . . . . . . . . . . . . . . . . . . . . . . . . . . . .

. . . . . . . . . . . . . . . . . . . . . . . . . . . . . . . . . . . . . . . . . . . .

. . . . . . . . . . . . . . . . . . . . . . . . . . . . . . . . . . . . . . . . . . . .

. . . . . . . . . . . . . . . . . . . . . . . . . . . . . . . . . . . . . . . . . . . .

. . . . . . . . . . . . . . . . . . . . . . . . . . . . . . . . . . . . . . . . . . . .

. . . . . . . . . . . . . . . . . . . . . . . . . . . . . . . . . . . . . . . . . . . .

. . . . . . . . . . . . . . . . . . . . . . . . . . . . . . . . . . . . . . . . . . . .

. . . . . . . . . . . . . . . . . . . . . . . . . . . . . . . . . . . . . . . . . . . .

. . . . . . . . . . . . . . . . . . . . . . . . . . . . . . . . . . . . . . . . . . . .

. . . . . . . . . . . . . . . . . . . . . . . . . . . . . . . . . . . . . . . . . . . .

. . . . . . . . . . . . . . . . . . . . . . . . . . . . . . . . . . . . . . . . . . . .

. . . . . . . . . . . . . . . . . . . . . . . . . . . . . . . . . . . . . . . . . . . .

# TWENTY-THREE

# Give up self-sabotage

*'Courage does not always roar. Sometimes courage is the quiet voice at the end of the day saying, "I will try again tomorrow."'*

Mary Anne Radmacher

My client Asim had a thing for luxury hotels. Instead of coming to me for coaching, his preference was to meet in a coffee shop of his choosing, usually in the foyer of a five-star hotel. While he savoured the surroundings, I listened to his updates with interest.

On one such occasion, we spoke about an upcoming talk he was due to give and he shared his apprehension about it. Despite his confidence, Asim, like most of us, confessed that public speaking wasn't his preference.

'The problem is, I sabotage myself,' he told me. 'I know weeks ahead of time that I need to prepare but I leave it until the day before and then I'm rushed and stressed and my performance isn't great.'

I didn't tell him at the time that this was one of my own ways of self-sabotaging too.

Over the ensuing years, I have come to discover that many of the methods of self-sabotage that clients use are ones I've tried myself.

Some psychologists suggest that our self-defeating behaviour is unconscious and related to low self-esteem or self-worth, and while this might be true for many of our goals, I believe self-sabotage is more nuanced than that. We sabotage our success for lighter reasons too.

We do it because we find certain tasks boring or repetitive. We do it when we're tired, overwhelmed or distracted. We sabotage ourselves when we don't have the discipline or the habit of sticking with a task that's difficult.

One way to recognise the drivers of your self-defeating behaviours is to imagine your goals in two categories.

Category one includes your long-term dreams. To write a children's book one day. To act in a play. To live overseas for a year. To share a deep and genuine connection with your partner. To live as the most authentic version of yourself. To become a leader in your field.

These are the goals we're likely to sabotage when self-esteem gets in the way. Our vigilant inner critic internalises the negative attitudes of parents and early caregivers as well as our own limiting beliefs and it tells us, 'There's no point in trying. You won't succeed anyway.'

Category two includes our short-term goals and our more imme-diate actions. To tidy the kitchen after breakfast. To finish my tax return. To cook a healthy meal. To return a phone call.

Our 'seemingly irrelevant decisions' (a term derived from treat-ment for addiction) play a significant role in inhibiting our success. You open your email and lose interest in tidying the kitchen. You access your tax file several times and become overwhelmed. You neglect to buy the ingredients for a healthy meal, so when you're hungry and tired, you call for pizza. You flick on the television, and then it's too late to call your friend.

We do these things not just because we don't value ourselves but because we've created habits that take us away from the uncomfortable feelings of boredom, overwhelm, impatience or apathy. Our preference is to seek behaviours that offer stimulation, entertainment or immediate reward.

In many ways, our self-defeating behaviours are the result of our hidden addictions. As psychology professor Brian Anderson argues, we're all addicted in some way – we just have different things we rely on to keep our unsettling thoughts at bay.

Anderson's theory is that even the healthiest people are 'wired' to do things that feel instantly rewarding and that sometimes those things are beyond our control. Because these habits are often outside our conscious awareness, it takes effort and hard work to overcome these habits and replace them with healthier options that move us towards our goals.

On closer reflection, Asim could see that this pattern of procrastinating was part of a bigger problem – he wanted to be taken more seriously at work and perceived as a leader. While the first issue was to overcome his habit of procrastinating, he was able to see that his limiting belief of 'I'm not good enough' needed addressing too.

Very often, we repeat our self-defeating patterns because we *expect to fail* or we *don't believe we deserve to succeed*. We hold ourselves back because we *feel we're not ready to show up in the world* or *not ready to put our creative work into the public arena*. Sometimes we choose self-defeating behaviours as a way of rebelling against perfection in what is otherwise a tightly controlled life. Or, like Asim, we might leave our preparation until the last minute to give ourselves a legitimate excuse for why our performance wasn't so great.

# How do you self-sabotage?

- Procrastinating
- Not staying focused or committed
- Distracting yourself with social media, television, etc.
- Hiding your strengths
- Running away
- Not asking for help
- Not being prepared
- Blaming others
- Not taking responsibility
- Not communicating your needs
- Overcommitting / overoptimism
- Burying your head in the sand / being in denial
- Not setting boundaries / not saying no
- Putting everyone else's needs before your own
- Numbing yourself when it gets too hard (food, alcohol, drugs)
- Creating conflict
- Overspending
- Excessive worry

# How to overcome self-sabotage

Regardless of your preferred way or ways to self-sabotage, the beginning point is to catch your inclination in the moment so you can choose a different behaviour.

## Be clear about what you're trying to achieve

Reflect back on the *best possible self* (pages 57–8) and *vision* (pages 66–7) exercises and if you haven't already done so, identify a few clear short-term goals. You may also find it helpful to map out how you would spend your time in your version of an ideal week. Draft a timetable for every day of the week and include all the important elements you would include to take care of your wellbeing, your relationships, your career and your home. Consider how and where in your week you could prioritise your most important goals. Are you currently scheduling these things? If not, what could you include?

## Become aware when you're sabotaging

Mindful awareness and self-compassion are key here. The idea is not to attack or criticise yourself when you discover your lack of focus, but rather to bring about a sense of open awareness when you find yourself distracted. 'Here I am procrastinating,' or 'Here I am opening the fridge door again.' If you can bring a spirit of lightness to the way you interact with yourself, you're less likely to get caught in the voice of the inner critic.

## Work out why you're doing it

Get to know your typical thinking styles. For example, if you're perfectionistic, you might notice that you become overwhelmed by your own extreme standards. If you're a people pleaser, you may find yourself saying yes to all requests without properly considering them. If you're inclined to anxiety, you may find that you numb yourself with food, alcohol, social media or online shopping. Try saying to yourself, 'This is my brain's way of sabotaging me.'

## Recognise it as draining

Sometimes we tell ourselves that we *need* the extra chocolate, the weekend on the sofa binge-watching television or the extra pair of shoes we can't really afford. Once we examine our habitual behaviours, we often find that despite the short-term relief they offer, these habits actually drain us and deplete us of energy.

## Tell yourself, 'I have a choice'

We all want to feel a sense of free will about the choices we make and sometimes we convince ourselves that our self-defeating behaviours *are our business*. The problem is, self-sabotage isn't really exercising free will at all. The behaviours that hold us back are often unconscious and habitual, and we engage in them without actively choosing to. They might help to mask our immediate pain but they also inhibit our long-term wellbeing. Once you have the awareness that these measures offer only short-term relief, you may find it easier to take back your sense of agency as you tell yourself, 'I have a choice here. If I want the chocolate, I can have it, but I know how I'll feel afterwards. I acknowledge I'm feeling flat this afternoon – I think a walk will be a better option.'

## Break your big tasks into smaller steps

When you're trying to tackle bigger goals, break them down into smaller, more manageable tasks and be realistic about how long each of these tasks will take. If you're like me and a persistent 'over-committer', recognise this pattern and allow a more realistic amount of time to get things done. You may find it helpful to create buffer zones. For example, if a piece of work is due on Friday, aim to have it fully completed by Wednesday.

## Change one habit at a time

It might be tempting to overhaul your entire life or rid yourself of all your unhelpful habits immediately. Set out with a realistic expectation so you're less likely to fail. Choose one habit and allow yourself room for imperfection.

## Get to know the rhythm of your day

Most people find that when they create a rhythm to their day and group tasks together, they're able to be more productive and focused. Get to know which times of day are best for different activities. You might prefer to email or exercise first thing in the morning; you may prefer to make phone calls or have meetings mid-morning; or you might want to keep a few hours clear each afternoon to focus on a more detailed piece of work. Tune in to your body's natural energy rhythms and regardless of your schedule, include several short breaks in your day.

## Ask for help when you need it

When a goal feels too big to tackle on your own, don't be too proud to reach out for help.

## Reward yourself or celebrate

Use your breaks to do something you enjoy such as taking yourself out for a coffee, calling a friend, spending a few hours painting, gardening or reading your book. At the end of a day or a week of focus, reward yourself with something that feels like a gift.

**What's one way you can give up self-sabotage this week?**

. . . . . . . . . . . . . . . . . . . . . . . . . . . . . . . . . . . . . . . . . . . . . . . .

. . . . . . . . . . . . . . . . . . . . . . . . . . . . . . . . . . . . . . . . . . . . . . . .

. . . . . . . . . . . . . . . . . . . . . . . . . . . . . . . . . . . . . . . . . . . . . . . .

. . . . . . . . . . . . . . . . . . . . . . . . . . . . . . . . . . . . . . . . . . . . . . . .

. . . . . . . . . . . . . . . . . . . . . . . . . . . . . . . . . . . . . . . . . . . . . . . .

**What's one way you could celebrate at the end of the week?**

. . . . . . . . . . . . . . . . . . . . . . . . . . . . . . . . . . . . . . . . . . . . . . . .

. . . . . . . . . . . . . . . . . . . . . . . . . . . . . . . . . . . . . . . . . . . . . . . .

. . . . . . . . . . . . . . . . . . . . . . . . . . . . . . . . . . . . . . . . . . . . . . . .

. . . . . . . . . . . . . . . . . . . . . . . . . . . . . . . . . . . . . . . . . . . . . . . .

. . . . . . . . . . . . . . . . . . . . . . . . . . . . . . . . . . . . . . . . . . . . . . . .

# TWENTY-FOUR

# Build your resilience

*'Clouds come floating into my life, no longer to carry rain or usher storm,*
*but to add color to my sunset sky.'*

Rabindranath Tagore

Some people in this world seem to be dealt a much tougher hand than any of us would consider reasonable.

Mary is one of those people. Three years after losing her mum to cancer at the age of eight, her older sister died by suicide. Mary then found herself fighting for her own life as a teenager when she was diagnosed with cancer. While chemotherapy and radiotherapy were brutal treatments for anyone, they did save her life. But, in her thirties when she and her husband tried to have children, she discovered the cancer treatment had left her infertile. Mary and her husband didn't have the funds to pursue adoption or IVF as a pathway to becoming parents and were shattered by the need to let go of that dream.

If most of us had to deal with life challenges like those Mary has faced, we can imagine them leaving us feeling worn down or even in despair. But Mary has a sunny disposition which means I always leave an interaction with her feeling better than I did at the start of the conversation.

Mary's positive attitude isn't simply a mask she wears to hide a huge well of pain. She really does approach life with an attitude of openness, gratitude and acceptance. Her resilience is something to behold.

# What is resilience?

Resilience isn't stoicism, indifference or resolute doggedness. It's not disconnection or hiding from emotions. And it's not the ability to shrug things off or make your way through life with a stiff upper lip.

Resilient people have the ability to cope with life's challenges when they're *in the midst of* those challenges and to *bounce back* after a huge challenge. They keep showing up in the face of extreme stress, anxiety or grief.

We don't need to experience significant or ongoing adversity in order to develop resilience. It's a trait we can all build, and a good time to start building it is when everything is smooth sailing.

# How to build your resilience

A simple model for resilience building comes from an Australian program and book of the same name, *The Resilience Project* by Hugh van Cuylenburg. Hugh's resilience model is based around three pillars that we've explored earlier – those of gratitude, empathy (kindness and compassion) and mindfulness.

As well as reflecting on the question Martin Seligman posed in his research, *'What are three things that went well for me today?'*, *The Resilience Project* suggests answering three additional questions each day:

- What was the best thing that happened to me today?
- Who am I most grateful for today and why?
- What am I looking forward to most about tomorrow?

If ever you've tried gratitude journalling and found it didn't work for you, it's likely that the question, *'What am I grateful for today?'* is too broad for you or that over time you've found that your answers become trite or repetitive.

*The Resilience Project's* questions draw instead on research that suggests people express gratitude in three ways:

- By referring to the past to reflect on positive memories
- Being in the present, without taking anything for granted
- Maintaining a positive outlook about the future

By answering these questions daily, you're likely to see an effect after 21 days and be three times more likely to notice the positive aspects in life.

Tens of thousands of years of evolution has meant the human brain is naturally wired to scan for danger and notice what's negative. When we were out on the savannah, we had to be mindful of wild animals and enemy tribes in order to stay alive, but this overvigilance means we interact with modern-day challenges less effectively.

As well as balancing this negative brain bias, maintaining a gratitude journal long-term offers other resilience-boosting benefits including higher levels of energy, better quality sleep and lower levels of depression and anxiety.

The second pillar of *The Resilience Project's* model is empathy. These qualities are easy to practise by demonstrating concern and understanding, or actively doing something kind for someone else.

When we do something nice for another person, we get an oxytocin boost which increases our energy, improves happiness and provides us with feelings of positivity. While it might feel selfish to do something for others with a view towards building your own resilience, the end result of kindness is that both the giver and receiver get a lift too.

Mary told me that people often try to stop her from doing things for them because they feel she has enough on her plate. She reassures them that it makes her feel good to be able to help. The boost she gets acts as a buffer against the things in her life that wear her resilience down.

Mindfulness is the final pillar of *The Resilience Project's* approach to building resilience. Being mindful takes many forms. A friend of mine, Kate, who lost her husband suddenly, told me how a very basic mindfulness practice got her through every day in the first few months after his death. She said:

Whenever my mind started casting ahead to next week, next month, next year and threatened to overwhelm me with thoughts of how on earth the kids and I could possibly do life without my husband, I brought myself back to the moment and had conversations with myself that looked like this:

*What are you doing right now?*

*Driving.*

*Where are you going?*

*To the shops.*

*What are you getting from the shops?*

*Some fruit for the kids' lunchboxes.*

And so on.

This is a beautiful demonstration of how you can use mindfulness in everyday life. It's the simple practice of bringing yourself back to the moment.

Beyond gratitude, empathy and mindfulness, there are a few other tools that help build resilience too.

## Get enough sleep

Given the significant effect a lack of sleep has on your ability to cope, it's important to prioritise sleep. Practise good sleep hygiene by setting regular bed and wake times. Participate in a regular relaxation regime such as meditating or listening to guided meditation tapes and/or create an evening ritual that allows you time to calm down.

As difficult as it can be, do your best not to stress about your sleep. Most people can manage well on around six hours sleep each night but we think that if we have less than eight, we'll be tired and unable to function. If you do wake in the middle of the night, worrying about getting back to sleep will make it more difficult to do so. While it might be ideal to leave your phone out of the bedroom, a guided meditation at this point might help you fall back into sleep.

## Exercise daily

Daily physical activity is something else that feeds good sleep habits as it ensures you're more physically tired at bedtime. It also directly lowers the level of stress hormones in your bloodstream (the ones that put your body into fight-or-flight mode), which means that physical activity has a double benefit when it comes to boosting resilience. Some researchers suggest that vigorous exercise late in the day can boost endorphins, making it a little harder to sleep, so play around with the best time of day for exercise for you.

# Find meaning

The final resilience booster is the ability to find meaning. Mark started his own mortgage broking business in his twenties and quickly achieved a level of success well beyond what he'd thought was possible. Within a couple of decades, he was happily married with two little girls and a life that felt pretty much perfect. Just after his 40th birthday, his good fortune changed when he had an unexpected falling-out with his business partner. Mark spent the next few years negotiating a difficult and financially painful exit from his business as well as coming to terms with the loss of a long-term friend.

Burnt out from the ongoing conflict and with his business confidence low, Mark was finding it hard to even get out of bed.

Later diagnosed with depression, Mark spent the next 12 months working closely with his GP and a psychologist. After a year, he still struggled with the shock of what had happened to him but he began to regain some of his confidence.

By the time Mark came to see me, he had started to explore how he could derive meaning from his experience. He had a sense that this would be the final part of his recovery. Mark began to research men's groups and eventually started a group of his own where he shared his experience and began mentoring others going through a life challenge.

For Mark, being able to give back helped him regain his sense of purpose. Despite the fact that the fear of his depression returning might always be there, he found the ability to keep moving forward in a meaningful way.

## Practise resilience

Resilience is underpinned by an attitude of openness, gratitude and acceptance. These are not *traits* that you either have or don't have, they are *mindsets* that need to be built, and you can start building them anytime.

Start with the simple *gratitude* practices described on page 167.

Find ways each day to be *kind*, both to others and yourself.

Incorporate moments of *mindfulness* into your days, and build up to a daily meditation practice. Take care of your wellbeing by getting enough sleep, incorporating exercise into your days and look for ways to find meaning in life.

**What's one change you can incorporate this week?**

. . . . . . . . . . . . . . . . . . . . . . . . . . . . . . . . . . . . . . . . . . . .

. . . . . . . . . . . . . . . . . . . . . . . . . . . . . . . . . . . . . . . . . . . .

. . . . . . . . . . . . . . . . . . . . . . . . . . . . . . . . . . . . . . . . . . . .

. . . . . . . . . . . . . . . . . . . . . . . . . . . . . . . . . . . . . . . . . . . .

. . . . . . . . . . . . . . . . . . . . . . . . . . . . . . . . . . . . . . . . . . . .

. . . . . . . . . . . . . . . . . . . . . . . . . . . . . . . . . . . . . . . . . . . .

. . . . . . . . . . . . . . . . . . . . . . . . . . . . . . . . . . . . . . . . . . . .

# TWENTY-FIVE

# Trust your intuition

*'The inspiration you seek is already within you. Be silent and listen.'*
Rumi, 13th-century Persian poet, scholar and mystic

Science has often been dismissive of the concept of intuition, but in recent years, researchers have found evidence to suggest that our intuition involves accessing information we store at a subconscious level. Many now believe that what we call our *gut feelings* are covert emotional memories that have made their way into our consciousness.

In his book *Blink*, Malcolm Gladwell introduced the idea of rapid cognition or 'thin slicing', which is essentially the ability to make rapid decisions based on tiny slivers of information. We make an assessment about a person we meet from spending just a few seconds with them; we move to a different part of the train because we 'sense' something's not right about someone we're sharing the carriage with; or we decide we won't accept a job offer moments into the interview process.

While 'thin-slicing' decisions aren't always positive (some snap judgements are influenced by pre-existing bias or prejudices), they can be enormously helpful.

When we need to make quick decisions, our split-second judgements are often beneficial. We unconsciously and rapidly sift through our internal files and reach a conclusion without knowing why we've reached it. The ability to find patterns and make quick decisions based on 'thin slices' of information is a fast and powerful form of intuitive thinking.

Unlike conscious reasoning, intuition is often experienced or sensed in the body and sometimes it doesn't seem entirely rational. When we're being intuitive, we're not engaging the analytical part of our brain but rather, we're listening to a deeper knowing that can guide us in the most unexpected and helpful ways.

For most people, listening to your intuition means guiding your awareness into your body and being curious and open to the information you intuit. It's about really listening to and trusting that inner knowing. When you connect with your intuition, you have the ability to *sense things* before you really *know them*, and often this knowing can't be easily explained.

When my daughter Meg had her son, Oscar, she was given lots of advice about how to parent him. 'Get him into a routine.' 'Let him cry it out.' 'Don't make a rod for your back.' Everyone had an opinion.

Without any experience in mothering and with a baby who didn't feed or sleep well, she had nowhere to turn but the 'experts'. Yet their advice left her hugely conflicted. She had a deep sense that this wasn't the kind of mother she wanted to be to her son.

In rare moments of quiet, she scoured the internet for different opinions. Guided by something she wasn't even aware of at the time, she kept searching until she eventually found stories of women who had resisted a rigid approach to sleeping and feeding. This was advice that resonated.

Meg's intuitive voice had told her something different about how she should parent this baby and she was wise enough to listen. Making the courageous decision to ignore other people, instead she chose to trust her gut instinct and tune in to the needs of her son.

Her approach was a mindful one. She slowed down and took the time to get to know her son. Feeding and getting him to sleep took a little longer than it did for other babies and called for nurturing and patience. She was able to ease him gently into a routine and this felt much more aligned with her values.

We all have the capacity to be intuitive, but there are times in our lives when we find it more difficult. When your mind is racing with thoughts, if you're anxious, stressed or overly busy, it's difficult to quieten your mind enough to tune in. If you're in an overly emotional state or under the influence of alcohol or drugs, it's also unlikely you'll be able to listen. But *not listening* is often something we do to ourselves – we ignore the little niggles when they're telling us things we'd rather not hear.

While your intuition can often protect you and keep you safe from harm, it can also be a positive alert, telling you to be open to a new relationship, to move to a new place or to take a job that sounds challenging.

If you've lost touch with your intuition, try the following things to help you reconnect.

## Spend time in stillness

A regular meditation practice is perhaps the most effective way to cultivate the kind of self-awareness that helps you connect with intuition. Even just a few minutes of quiet reflection at the beginning of each day will help you to become more aware of the wisdom that resides within.

Regardless of whether you're meditating or not, try to spend some time each week without any distractions or entertainment. If possible, get into nature to lower your cortisol levels and to help you feel grounded. When you're able to evoke a greater sense of physical relaxation, you'll find it easier to be aware of your gut instinct.

## Listen to your body

Once you become more practised at tuning in, you'll start to notice that often, within seconds of meeting someone new, or when you walk into certain physical spaces, you'll get a certain 'feeling' about them.

Many people report that they have this sensation in their belly area (it's why we call it our 'gut feeling' or 'gut instinct'). Our enteric nervous system, which is lined with one hundred million neurons, is constantly sending messages back to the brain. And while the jury's still out on exactly how this system affects our thoughts, your brain is certainly impacted by your gut (and vice versa). Try not to ignore these instincts or rationalise your way out of them. Listen in and be curious about the wisdom your body is offering.

It's sometimes easier in hindsight to see when you had an intuitive hunch and when you didn't act on it. If this happens, don't beat yourself up for not acknowledging your insight at the time, but tune your radar so it's more sharply focused on instinctual warnings in the future.

## Let your subconscious guide you while you're asleep

Spend a couple of weeks paying attention to your dreams. Keep a notebook beside your bed and upon waking, jot down whatever elements of your dream you remember. Even just a sentence or two is a good start. Recall how you were feeling in your dream and think about how those feelings show up in your everyday life. Consider also that the characters in your dreams might represent different aspects of yourself. While it's tempting to look to a dream analyst to decipher your dreams, try tuning in to your own interpretations first. You know yourself better than anyone and with an open and curious mind, it's likely you'll learn to understand some of the messages on your own.

## Tap into the transition between wakefulness and sleep

Sometimes our sleepy subconscious mind will guide us in ways we're less open to when we're using our rational, waking mind. The brief transition between wakefulness and sleep (a state known as hypnagogia) is a time where we often find a moment of clarity or discover the answer to a problem that feels inherently right. It's not always easy to catch this time because it's so brief, but if you're interested to learn more about it, read up about how Albert Einstein and Salvador Dalí tapped into this fascinating state to guide them in their work.

## Give yourself time to pause

When you do have a strong intuitive thought, it doesn't mean you need to rush into a decision. You may want to research your choices more thoroughly or you might prefer to just sit on your decision for a day or two. While you're in this state of flux, it might be tempting to ask friends and family for their opinion. Instead, keep tuning in so you learn to trust what feels right for you.

## Is it fear or is it intuition?

Sometimes it's difficult to determine the difference between intuition and self-doubt or fear. You'll find it easiest to connect with genuine intuition when you're in a state of calm, not in a highly excited or emotional state. If you're fairly relaxed and still uncertain, try to break your decision into the smallest possible parts and ask yourself, 'What does my intuition tell me about this aspect of the decision?' Be curious about your fears too. Write each of them down and ask yourself how you might overcome the worst-case scenario in each one. It's likely you'll find your intuition a good guide here as well.

**Where have you ignored your intuition?**

. . . . . . . . . . . . . . . . . . . . . . . . . . . . . . . . . . . . . . . . . . . . . . . . . .

. . . . . . . . . . . . . . . . . . . . . . . . . . . . . . . . . . . . . . . . . . . . . . . . . .

. . . . . . . . . . . . . . . . . . . . . . . . . . . . . . . . . . . . . . . . . . . . . . . . . .

. . . . . . . . . . . . . . . . . . . . . . . . . . . . . . . . . . . . . . . . . . . . . . . . . .

. . . . . . . . . . . . . . . . . . . . . . . . . . . . . . . . . . . . . . . . . . . . . . . . . .

. . . . . . . . . . . . . . . . . . . . . . . . . . . . . . . . . . . . . . . . . . . . . . . . . .

. . . . . . . . . . . . . . . . . . . . . . . . . . . . . . . . . . . . . . . . . . . . . . . . . .

. . . . . . . . . . . . . . . . . . . . . . . . . . . . . . . . . . . . . . . . . . . . . . . . . .

. . . . . . . . . . . . . . . . . . . . . . . . . . . . . . . . . . . . . . . . . . . . . . . . . .

# TWENTY-SIX

# Face your fears

*'At any moment, you have a choice, that either leads you closer to your spirit or further away from it.'*

Thích Nhất Hạnh, Vietnamese monk

In 2014 Jim Carrey delivered a commencement address to the Maharishi University of Management that was as poignant as it was funny. This part has always stuck with me:

> *Now fear is going to be a player in your life. But you get to decide how much. You can spend your whole life imagining ghosts, worrying about the pathway to the future, but all there will ever be is what's happening here, in the decisions we make in this moment, which are based in either love or fear. So many of us choose our path out of fear disguised as practicality.*

The sentiment of that last line was certainly true for Andy when a change in work situation saw him move to a new city where he didn't know another soul. Andy was incredibly shy and it took him a long time to form the friendships he had in his hometown. The thought of 'starting again from scratch' was so exhausting he chose a path out of fear disguised as practicality. He decided he'd throw himself into his new job and work long hours so he'd be too tired and time-poor to feel lonely.

The problem with letting fear make decisions for us is that it prevents us from making meaningful change in our lives. In order to grow and evolve, we need to become more comfortable with the discomfort of facing our fears.

It takes courage to face our fears, a strength some of us believe we're not armed with.

Stanley Rachman, a psychologist at the University of British Columbia, has a different approach to courage. He's also a leading expert on fear. After studying people engaged in some of the world's most dangerous professions, he came to the conclusion that the concept of courage is quite misunderstood. Many of us define courage and bravery as 'fearlessness'. Rachman proposes that courage is not the *absence of fear*; rather, it is the decision to *move forward in spite of fear*.

In other words, the people we consider to be brave aren't impervious to fear. They see it and acknowledge it, but don't allow it to stop them in their tracks.

How can we tap into this ability to sit with the discomfort of being scared and move forward anyway?

We can start with *understanding what we're really scared of.*

Andy thought his biggest fear was the fear of being lonely so he devised what he thought was an effective management plan: to work more in order to avoid loneliness. In reality, his biggest fear was having to meet new people. His social anxiety meant he overthought every interaction he had with people he wasn't comfortable around and was constantly fearful of being judged harshly by those people.

The next step is to *accept that the fear is there*.

When we're fearful of something, our immediate impulse is to either run away from the fear or try to talk ourselves out of it. Neither of these methods is particularly effective because they create anxiety which exacerbates the feelings of fear. What *is* effective is accepting the fear. It's real. It's there and we don't need to pretend that it's not.

Once Andy normalised his fears around meeting new people, he was in a position to take the next step, *facing up to those fears* – managing them in a way that allowed him to move forward.

One of my favourite exercises to do with clients in this regard is Cheryl Richardson's 'Face Your Fear' game.

The game offers seven categories and requires you to complete an exercise from each of the categories over the course of 30 days. Those categories are:

- Fulfil a secret dream
- Stand out from the crowd
- Tell the truth
- Be bold
- Face a physical fear
- Face a professional fear
- Face a financial fear

You get to choose how 'big' or 'small' you go with the above.

To fulfil a secret dream, you might book a holiday to somewhere you've always wanted to go, or you might download a language app on your phone and commit to spending 15 minutes a day learning that language.

To stand out from the crowd you might put a streak of colour through your hair, wear a brightly coloured shirt when you otherwise wouldn't or decide to speak up in a meeting.

Telling the truth might look like apologising to a family member for hurting their feelings or correcting some information that's not quite true on your resume.

Being bold could mean something as simple as complimenting a stranger, or as scary (but satisfying) as accepting the chance to be interviewed on the radio.

Facing a physical fear can be quite confronting. Many of my clients put 'booking a dentist appointment' in this category but it can also involve engaging in a team sport, training and competing in a fun run or even joining a yoga class.

To face a professional fear, you might ask your boss for a promotion or a raise at your next performance review. Or maybe you could sell yourself more effectively in an interview or in your LinkedIn profile.

Financial fears are another area most people find challenging. Starting small might involve something as simple as opening your internet banking and simply looking at the balance on your accounts. Others make a budget and resolve to stick to it for 30 days.

The beauty of this 'Face Your Fear' game is that it allows you to build courage by gradually exposing yourself to small acts that are outside your comfort zone. These are the same things that build your confidence and emotional strength naturally over time. Another way of thinking about this is that courage and confidence come from 'couraging', not from changing the way that you think.

Before tackling Andy's fear of meeting and interacting with new people, he practised the exercise above for a month. When we eventually turned our attention to broadening his social circle, Andy was operating with a small boost in confidence and a greater sense of emotional strength.

Andy had been invited to join his colleagues for lunch on several occasions but he had previously turned those offers down. The next time he was asked, Andy said yes and while he mostly listened as others in the group spoke, he felt he'd taken a big step forward by simply being there.

Later, he joined a soccer game organised by his work team and the confidence Andy gained from these small social interactions with workmates made him think that he could try something similar outside of his work. His apartment building had a fitness studio in it, so he paid for three months in advance to ensure he gave it a good go.

Initially, Andy kept to himself but he noted how friendly and encouraging the instructors and his fellow exercisers were. Towards the end of the second month, he heard about a fitness challenge the studio was running, which included a social event for all the participants at the end. He resolved to take on the challenge and attend the function, even though it filled him with fear.

Andy had previously told me that having just one person he knew at a social function made all the difference to his anxiety levels. I encouraged him to use the eight-week period of the fitness challenge to connect with just one person, instead of trying to make a dozen new friends.

This strategy worked. While Andy focused on creating a single connection, he made several new acquaintances over the course of the following few weeks. When the end-of-challenge function rolled around, he was still nervous about attending. But in the end, the hardest part was walking into the room. Once he'd located 'his people' – the new friends he'd made – he was able to relax and enjoy the night.

Andy's story is a reminder that facing our fears is a process. Bravery is not a light bulb that can be turned on or off with the flick of a switch. Building courage *is* like building a muscle – the more you exercise it, the stronger it gets. Small actions repeated often will strengthen that muscle more than one giant feat of courage that never gets repeated.

**Challenge yourself over the coming month by engaging in Cheryl Richardson's 'Face Your Fear' game.**
I will fulfil the following secret dream. . . . . . . . . . . . . . . . . . . . . . . .
To stand out in the crowd I will . . . . . . . . . . . . . . . . . . . . . . . . . . . .
I will tell the truth by . . . . . . . . . . . . . . . . . . . . . . . . . . . . . . . . . .
I will take a bold step by. . . . . . . . . . . . . . . . . . . . . . . . . . . . . . . . .
To face a physical fear I will . . . . . . . . . . . . . . . . . . . . . . . . . . . . . .
To face a professional fear I will . . . . . . . . . . . . . . . . . . . . . . . . . . . .
To face a financial fear I will. . . . . . . . . . . . . . . . . . . . . . . . . . . . . . .

# TWENTY-SEVEN

# Find your tribe

*'The human soul doesn't want to be advised or fixed or saved. It simply
wants to be witnessed – to be seen, heard and companioned exactly as it is.'*
Parker Palmer, *On Being* podcast

While the physical threats from solo living and isolation are not as
real today as they were 30,000 years ago, current research shows how
deeply wired we are for the need to belong. Matthew Lieberman,
scientist and author of *Social – Why Our Brains Are Wired to Connect*,
suggests that our need to connect is as fundamental as our need for
food and water.

His research has shown that social pain (felt in the face of exclusion
and rejection, for example) is experienced through the same pathways
our brains use to process physical pain. In other words, we feel
rejection as a very real pain, not just a psychological one.

Studies on loneliness have shown that our brains go into a hypervigilant mode when we feel socially isolated. This means we're more
likely to see danger whether it's there or not, we're at higher risk of
fragmented sleep and we're more inclined to experience depressive

symptoms. Loneliness creates a negative loop because when we're in self-preservation mode, we become very self-focused and less able to experience perspective and empathy, which further affects our ability to connect.

Strong social connections boost our mental and physical health and improve our quality of life. Studies have shown that a sense of belonging can strengthen your immune system, help you recover from disease and even lengthen your life.

In order to find these connections when we don't have them in our lives currently and to do so without feeling desperate, we need to extend some kindness to ourselves.

Loneliness and the sense of 'not belonging' make us more susceptible to negative feelings, and one of the strongest negative feelings is shame. Shame makes us feel powerless and worthless which severely hampers our ability to reach out and make meaningful connections with others.

Gently acknowledging your loneliness and allowing yourself to feel it without applying any judgement to yourself will reduce the sense of desperation or entitlement that can colour the interactions we seek to combat loneliness.

Once you've done that, the next step is to understand the kind of connections that you're seeking.

No single 'tribe' will fulfil all your needs. You may love catching up with friends from school, but if your friends are all married with children and you're not, it's easy for that connection to feel isolating. You might be fortunate to have a close and loving family, but if everyone in your family is heavily into sport and you're the lone art lover, you're going to need to find your creative connections elsewhere.

Once you have a good understanding of the kind of connections that are missing from your life, the next step is to be realistic about the limitations you are facing. This can be a little tricky as it's sometimes hard to discern between a genuine limitation and an excuse that's based in fear.

My client Anica is an ambitious business owner who has a great relationship with her family and a loving husband she feels deeply connected with, but working on her own, she misses a workplace tribe.

When I first met with her, Anica's business was going through a huge growth phase and she was working 60 hours a week. She preciously guarded the hours outside of work as time to be with her husband. While she loved the idea of joining business groups where she would have the opportunity to meet with other business owners, she found it difficult to justify the time commitment. Also, as an introvert who spent her whole day speaking with people, she found the thought of extra in-person interactions exhausting.

After giving herself space and time to reflect, Anica was comfortable these were genuine limitations rather than excuses and she recognised that these limitations weren't a problem because they offered her boundaries within which to work.

Once you know the kind of connections you need and have an understanding of the limitations and challenges you have to work around, you can be intentional about where you go to seek out those connections.

Anica was clear that she wanted to meet other business owners, but not in a way that compromised the time she spent with her husband. She joined a business mentoring group where all the interaction was via an online forum. This gave her access to people who were experiencing the same challenges as she was and were able to support her through those challenges, while also inspiring her with their energy and ideas.

She started attending a three-day business conference each year where she got to see and chat with the people from the online group in real life. She loved how the in-person interactions added an extra dimension to the relationships she had created online. Anica was so impressed by how this tribe was able to fill a very specific hole in her life, she was inspired to start a similar online group for business owners with babies when her first child arrived.

We find connections wherever the people with the same interests as us spend time.

If you have a passion for creativity, you'll find 'your people' in art classes, at gallery openings or at art appreciation events. If you love fitness, you are likely to find people with the same values as you in the gym or exercise classes. Volunteering is another great way to meet people with similar interests. Many conferences require volunteers, as do most charities and even major sporting events.

You know you've found your tribe when you're with a group of people where you feel you belong. And key to belonging is knowing that people accept you and appreciate you for who you are. If you feel you're constantly being judged or you notice yourself changing your behaviour in order to fit in, then there's a good chance those people are not your tribe. If you find yourself feeling energised after an interaction, there's a good chance they are.

It's also important to remember that not all tribes last forever. As we evolve and as our life circumstances change, so too will the connection we have with the groups we are part of. Anica found that once she had kids, she spent more time in the business group she created for business owners with babies and less with the original group she'd joined. Then, when her children started school and she sold her business, she found new groups of 'her people' via volunteering at school and at the surf club her kids were part of.

## Use the EASE approach

The EASE acronym offered up by social neuroscientist John Cacioppo is a helpful reminder of how we can ease our way towards meaningful, affirming connections.

The first E stands for 'extend yourself'. This acknowledges that finding our tribe might require us to step outside our comfort zone and we can do that slowly and in a way that feels safe rather than feeling we have to throw ourselves into new interactions with abandon.

A is for 'action plan'. It can be easy to fall into the trap of thinking that serendipity and chance are the best way to make new friends and find people who 'get us'. While it would be nice if serendipity always provided for us, the reality is that sometimes it doesn't. More often than not, we need to take matters into our own hands.

S is for 'seek collectives', which refers to looking for people who have similar interests and values to you or who do similar activities.

Finally, the last E is for 'expect the best'. Remember, when we feel lonely, we are hypervigilant in looking out for threats. Any perceived rejection from someone we're seeking connection with will exacerbate this. If we can remind ourselves to expect the best from people, that hypervigilance can be taken down a few notches.

**Where might you find your tribe?**

. . . . . . . . . . . . . . . . . . . . . . . . . . . . . . . . . . . . . . . . . . . . . . .
. . . . . . . . . . . . . . . . . . . . . . . . . . . . . . . . . . . . . . . . . . . . . . .
. . . . . . . . . . . . . . . . . . . . . . . . . . . . . . . . . . . . . . . . . . . . . . .
. . . . . . . . . . . . . . . . . . . . . . . . . . . . . . . . . . . . . . . . . . . . . . .
. . . . . . . . . . . . . . . . . . . . . . . . . . . . . . . . . . . . . . . . . . . . . . .

# TWENTY-EIGHT

# Practise forgiveness

*'You hold in your hand an invitation: to remember the transforming power of forgiveness and loving kindness. To remember that no matter where you are and what you face, within your heart peace is possible.'*

Jack Kornfield

There will be times in all our lives where someone causes us hurt and pain. And there will be times where we cause hurt and pain to others, often unintentionally. While it might appear that we're able to keep moving forward despite the emotional scars of those times, when we dig deeper, we sometimes find that our inability to forgive ourselves or forgive the people who hurt us is holding us back from making meaningful change in our lives.

This was certainly the case for Maeve, who came to me for help understanding why she was having trouble forming strong female friendships. When we traced things back, she shared the story of how in her final year of primary school, she and her best friend had been separated at the wish of the other girl's mother and the

241

friendship had broken down. Since that time, she'd laboured under the belief that she wasn't a worthy or valuable friend. As a result, she felt scared about being open or vulnerable. When friendships began to get close, Maeve pulled away.

Jason was also having trouble with relationships, but of the romantic kind. Similar to Maeve, every time he found himself getting close to a partner, he'd subconsciously sabotage things. Jason suspected his parents' divorce had something to do with this, but he wasn't entirely sure about how to change his feelings or his behaviour.

In both Maeve and Jason's cases, forgiveness was key. They needed to let go of the past by forgiving themselves and the people who had hurt them.

Forgiving someone doesn't mean denying that something hurtful has happened to you. It's not about forgetting hurtful behaviour or condoning it and it's not even necessarily about reconciling with the person who hurt you.

Forgiveness is a conscious decision to let go of feelings of resentment towards someone who has caused you pain. You may not feel that they *deserve* your forgiveness, but forgiving is something you do for yourself. It's a chance to find inner peace rather than seeking justice and an opportunity to let go of your hurt instead of allowing it to define you.

If you're finding it difficult to let go, you might be experiencing one or more of the three common barriers to forgiveness.

The first is unreadiness. If you are still in a place of great emotional pain over a hurt that's been caused to you and you feel unable to shift your perspective to the wider view needed to move forward, it may be that you're not ready to forgive yet. And that's okay. Time and space are necessary in order to process your experience in a way that will allow forgiveness to occur. You may need to explore and under-stand your emotions more deeply, you may need time and space to properly grieve or maybe you just need to allow some healing to occur before you're ready to forgive.

The second barrier to forgiveness is self-protection, or the fear that after forgiving someone, they will cause you unbearable hurt again. Research has shown that people who feel they have a sense of control in a situation are more likely to forgive. Setting strong boundaries around behaviours you will accept from others will help you feel a greater sense of agency.

The third barrier is the need to save face. It is human nature to not want to appear weak or vulnerable. Refusing to 'give in' (which is what many of us mistakenly consider forgiveness to mean) allows us to exert control over a situation in which we otherwise feel power-less. Someone stuck behind this barrier generally needs to work on their self-esteem and self-worth. This will help you to find the emotional capacity required to forgive someone without feeling as though you've lost face.

When I started working with both Maeve and Jason, the first thing we needed to understand was if they were in *a place to contem-plate forgiveness*.

Happily, none of the above barriers were present so we could move forward to the second step, which is: *understanding who wins when we forgive*.

Malachy McCourt once said, 'Resentment is like taking poison and waiting for the other person to die.' When we hold on to resent-ment, we're the ones who suffer the most. Conversely, when we let go of that resentment, we are the ones who benefit the most.

The third step in the process of forgiveness is *understanding who you need to forgive.*

Maeve found she needed to forgive both her old friend for the hurt that was caused, but also herself for carrying the shame of that rejection around for so long. Similarly, Jason had to forgive his parents for getting divorced, but he also had to forgive himself for the fact that he always believed he was the reason for their divorce.

Sometimes the people we need to forgive may not deserve our forgiveness. It may also feel irrelevant to forgive ourselves for something we didn't do. (Jason, for example, was not responsible for his parents' divorce.) But, whether we think forgiveness is warranted or deserved, it's important to remember that it's the key to being able to move on from and let go of things that are holding us back – and we do this for ourselves, not for other people.

Once we know *who* we need to forgive, we need to find a way to actually do so.

A simple exercise is to visualise your feelings of resentment as a balloon you're holding on to. Then visualise yourself letting that balloon go. Research has shown the act of forgiveness elevates moods, enhances optimism and guards against anger, stress, anxiety and depression.

# Forgive yourself

Rick Hanson has a simple exercise that's helpful for forgiving ourselves. He recommends that you choose one area of your life you've been self-critical about, beginning with something small. For example, perhaps you've had a minor conflict with someone you care about. With that event in mind, work through the following statements.

Begin by connecting with your Inner Supporter. An easy way to do this is to think about someone who cares for you and imagine you can connect with that sense of caring from them.

As you reflect on yourself from the place of your Inner Supporter, make a list of some of your good qualities, such as 'patience', 'kindness', 'fairness', etc.

Acknowledge the facts of what happened.

In an honest way, take responsibility for your faults. Say in your mind or out loud (or write):

*I am responsible for* . . . . . . . . . . . . . . . . . , . . . . . . . . . . . . . . . .
*and* . . . . . . . . . . . . . . . . . . . . . . . . . . . . . . . . . . . . . . . . . . . . .

Be aware of the emotions that arise and give yourself permission to feel them.

Next, make a note of what you're not responsible for, such as misinterpretations and other people's overreactions.

*But I am NOT responsible for* . . . . . . . . , . . . . . . . . . . . . . . .
*and* . . . . . . . . . . . . . . . . . . . . . . . . . . . . . . . . . . . . . . . . . . . . .

Let the relief of what you're not responsible for sink in.

Next, decide what, if anything, remains to be done, either within yourself or out in the world. And if you can, go ahead and do that.

Next, actively forgive yourself. Say in your mind, out loud, in writing, or perhaps to others, statements like:

*I forgive myself for . . . . . . . . . . . . . . . . . , . . . . . . . . . . . . . . . .*
*and . . . . . . . . . . . . . . . . . . . . . . . . . . . . . . . . . . . . . . . . . . . .*
*I have taken responsibility and done what I could to make things better.*

I walked Maeve and Jason through this exercise. Here's what it looked like for Jason.

*I am responsible for carrying the feelings of shame and responsibility for my parents' divorce into my romantic relationships as an adult.*

*But I am not responsible for my parents' divorce.*

*I forgive myself for carrying those feelings of shame and resentment with me for so many years without questioning the validity of those feelings. I have taken responsibility for those feelings and sought the help of therapy to help me understand, process and let go of those feelings so they don't continue to impact future relationships.*

Both Maeve and Jason found forgiveness to be an incredibly powerful and freeing exercise. They took confidence from the fact that it was a tool they could call on whenever resentment threatened to weigh them down or affect the quality of their relationships with themselves or other people.

**Who do you need to forgive?**

. . . . . . . . . . . . . . . . . . . . . . . . . . . . . . . . . . . . . . . . . .

. . . . . . . . . . . . . . . . . . . . . . . . . . . . . . . . . . . . . . . . . .

. . . . . . . . . . . . . . . . . . . . . . . . . . . . . . . . . . . . . . . . . .

. . . . . . . . . . . . . . . . . . . . . . . . . . . . . . . . . . . . . . . . . .

. . . . . . . . . . . . . . . . . . . . . . . . . . . . . . . . . . . . . . . . . .

. . . . . . . . . . . . . . . . . . . . . . . . . . . . . . . . . . . . . . . . . .

. . . . . . . . . . . . . . . . . . . . . . . . . . . . . . . . . . . . . . . . . .

. . . . . . . . . . . . . . . . . . . . . . . . . . . . . . . . . . . . . . . . . .

. . . . . . . . . . . . . . . . . . . . . . . . . . . . . . . . . . . . . . . . . .

. . . . . . . . . . . . . . . . . . . . . . . . . . . . . . . . . . . . . . . . . .

. . . . . . . . . . . . . . . . . . . . . . . . . . . . . . . . . . . . . . . . . .

. . . . . . . . . . . . . . . . . . . . . . . . . . . . . . . . . . . . . . . . . .

. . . . . . . . . . . . . . . . . . . . . . . . . . . . . . . . . . . . . . . . . .

. . . . . . . . . . . . . . . . . . . . . . . . . . . . . . . . . . . . . . . . . .

. . . . . . . . . . . . . . . . . . . . . . . . . . . . . . . . . . . . . . . . . .

. . . . . . . . . . . . . . . . . . . . . . . . . . . . . . . . . . . . . . . . . .

. . . . . . . . . . . . . . . . . . . . . . . . . . . . . . . . . . . . . . . . . .

. . . . . . . . . . . . . . . . . . . . . . . . . . . . . . . . . . . . . . . . . .

. . . . . . . . . . . . . . . . . . . . . . . . . . . . . . . . . . . . . . . . . .

. . . . . . . . . . . . . . . . . . . . . . . . . . . . . . . . . . . . . . . . . .

. . . . . . . . . . . . . . . . . . . . . . . . . . . . . . . . . . . . . . . . . .

. . . . . . . . . . . . . . . . . . . . . . . . . . . . . . . . . . . . . . . . . .

. . . . . . . . . . . . . . . . . . . . . . . . . . . . . . . . . . . . . . . . . .

. . . . . . . . . . . . . . . . . . . . . . . . . . . . . . . . . . . . . . . . . .

. . . . . . . . . . . . . . . . . . . . . . . . . . . . . . . . . . . . . . . . . .

# TWENTY-NINE

# Did you choose the right dream?

*'Wanderer, there is no road, the road is made by walking.'*

Antonio Machado

For as long as Claire could remember, she wanted to work as a park ranger. Growing up in a country town where her parents were passionate bushwalkers and conservationists, she spent most of her school holidays camping and hiking and learning about the environment.

During her school years, she worked hard at her science subjects so she could secure a place in an environmental science degree. While she was still at uni, Claire found work experience as a Seasonal Park Ranger in her local shire and after finishing her degree, she secured a full-time job in her chosen field.

After almost a decade working in her dream role, Claire started to think she'd made the wrong choice. She loved spending time outdoors but she recognised that in putting all her energy into a single interest, she was missing the opportunity to do other things.

~

Even clients like Claire, who feel that they have clarity about a chosen career path, can reach a point where they question if they're in the right role. While she shared her parents' passion for the land, Claire came to realise that it was time for a change, so she could explore some new passions of her own.

## Did you choose your own dreams?

Take some time to think about your most closely held career and life dreams. Are they truly your own?

In the table below, make a note of all the people who have influenced your choices in each of the listed areas. You may find that as well as inspiring you in positive ways by acting as a role model or involving you in interests of their own, influence may have been negative. For example, family members or friends may have rejected some of your choices or maybe you rebelled in some way, in turn pushing away something you actually love.

| Life area | Who has influenced me most? |
|---|---|
| Career | |
| Partner relationship | |
| Friendships | |
| Family | |
| Health | |

| Finances | |
| --- | --- |
| Interests | |
| Lifestyle/location | |
| Spirituality | |
| Contribution | |

Look back across your list and consider whether you've chosen your dreams in order to live up to or rebel against someone else's expectations of you, rather than being true to yourself. Then ask yourself, what would you choose if you weren't worried about what other people think?

## Let them inspire you

My client Danielle spent her adult life working long hours in her family's business. Now that her parents were retired, she and her husband provided for her mum and dad, too, so she felt deeply loyal to the values instilled by family.

When we first met, Danielle shared that she had a complex relationship with money and found people who owned luxury goods quite showy and pretentious. Like her parents, who came from humble beginnings and valued hard work, Danielle and her husband often spoke critically about people with money. 'They're shallow and vacuous,' they told their kids.

Over several months, Danielle and I started to explore the origins of her feelings about money. Eventually, she told me she felt embarrassed to admit that there was part of her that envied people who owned beautiful things. She confessed she had a long-held secret dream of buying herself a few beautiful pieces of clothing – something she had never admitted to anyone and felt guilty about because she knew it clashed with her family's values.

Danielle felt that to be a good person, she should deny herself anything extravagant. Tapping into her parents' values of having a solid 'work ethic' and 'making sacrifices', she believed it would be wrong to aspire to any kind of material affluence.

When we looked at Danielle's personal values, we saw that as well as caring about hard work and being willing to give to the family, she held a secret value of 'aesthetic appreciation'. In her own words, this value, that had long been suppressed, reflected a desire to surround herself with things that were pleasing to her senses rather than wanting material possessions as a measure of status.

Uncovering your subconscious desires and dreams can sometimes mean challenging long-held values, beliefs or judgements. Those beliefs may have served to protect you from a sense of disappointment or even shame that you haven't yet been able to reconcile those goals with what you believe to be 'right' or 'good' or 'achievable'.

Turn your attention back to the people you consider role models (from the *values* and *best possible self* exercises on pages 24–8 and 66–7). You may like to reflect on people you admire or even envy. Sometimes we suppress feelings of jealousy because we feel that they're shameful emotions but the people who push our buttons in this way often have something to teach us. What is it about them that you admire or envy? What is it about their lifestyle that appeals to you? And what have you been telling yourself about why you can't or shouldn't aspire to or have those things?

Sometimes we hold others in high regard for their external achievements but we might also think of them in favourable terms for other values they express or for certain characteristics they embody.

For example, in the 'partner relationship' category, you might admire a couple who make time for a date night or who make each other laugh. In the 'interests' category you might idolise someone who is adventurous or creative, even if you don't see these qualities in yourself yet. Or like Danielle, you may feel both inspired and conflicted when you meet someone who values herself enough to buy a beautiful dress.

As you complete your responses in the following table, put aside any self-judgement and allow yourself to be completely honest with your answers. Open your mind to all the people you admire, even if that admiration is tinged with some envy.

| Life area | Who do I admire and for which achievements or qualities? |
|---|---|
| Career | |
| Partner relationship | |
| Friendships | |
| Family | |
| Health | |
| Finances | |

| Interests | |
|---|---|
| Lifestyle/location | |
| Spirituality | |
| Contribution | |

## You can modify your dream

When Danielle completed the above exercise, it was clear to her that she felt envious of people who felt free to express their love of beauty. She modified her vision to include a version of herself as someone who valued her appearance enough to enjoy her new interest in fashion and she added a section to reflect her ideal home – a place where her value of family happiness was frequently expressed but that also included a modest but tasteful renovation to her home.

## What if you choose the wrong path?

We often have the sense that there's one 'best' way to achieve success and that it usually involves a linear path with clearly mapped-out steps resulting in a greater sense of happiness or quality of life. We imagine that as we mature, our relationships will get easier, our income and asset base will grow, our career expertise will improve, and we'll be able to rectify with our own children the parenting errors our parents made with us.

We admire role models who appear to have direct paths to success, but we don't always reflect on the fact that the mistakes and setbacks they encountered along the way, helped to shape them as people and build their resilience too.

Your life path is likely to be meandering: it will include a few forward steps and some backward ones too. Over the course of time, hopefully you'll make progress in the direction of your dreams, but it's also very likely there'll be mistakes and missteps along the way – as well as the potential for a change in your course.

Regardless of what you choose at any given point in your life, there's no such thing as the *wrong* choice. This is just the direction you have chosen *for now*. You may not want to stay on this path forever but every experience you have will contribute to the wisdom you accumulate along the way. You may even find, as many people do, that your biggest mistakes will become life's most important enriching and meaningful lessons.

Regardless of whether your mistakes are a small error of judgement (such as dating the wrong person for a few months) or a more significant blunder (such as marrying into an unhappy relationship), it's also useful to remember that every poor decision can be reversed in some way.

The best you can do at any point in your life is to reconnect with your values and ask yourself, *is this the right life choice for now?*

## There might be some longing

Many years ago, a wise colleague told me that regardless of what we choose in our lives, it's likely that we'll still yearn for the things we don't have. 'There will always be some longing,' he told me. In something of a paradox, I found great comfort in this.

When Chris and I finally made it to our dream home, it felt anything but dreamlike. Here we were in an uninsulated, unrenovated house, with no friends nearby and with a cancer diagnosis to deal with. This wasn't at all what we'd envisaged.

I wished my friends were closer. I missed the familiarity of the home we had lovingly renovated over 25 years. I longed to sit in my cosy little kitchen with the afternoon sun streaming in.

There were many times over that cold winter that I questioned if we'd made the right move. Until I reminded myself of my colleague's words. When we lived in the city, we longed for a life in the country, and now, on the difficult days, I longed for the city and the security of all that was familiar and easy.

We made it through those months and the extra trials life threw at us. Chris eventually recovered and the following autumn, we gave the house a coat of paint, took up the 80s carpet and took down the beige curtains, planted veggies in the garden and we made our house feel like home. It was the right dream – it just took us a while to get there.

**Choose one action**

Would you change your dream if you adopted some of the qualities of the people you most admire?

. . . . . . . . . . . . . . . . . . . . . . . . . . . . . . . . . . . . . . . . . . . . . . . .

. . . . . . . . . . . . . . . . . . . . . . . . . . . . . . . . . . . . . . . . . . . . . . . .

. . . . . . . . . . . . . . . . . . . . . . . . . . . . . . . . . . . . . . . . . . . . . . . .

. . . . . . . . . . . . . . . . . . . . . . . . . . . . . . . . . . . . . . . . . . . . . . . .

. . . . . . . . . . . . . . . . . . . . . . . . . . . . . . . . . . . . . . . . . . . . . . . .

# THIRTY

# Make your life beautiful now

*'Be soft. Do not let the world make you hard. Do not let the bitterness steal your sweetness. Take pride that even though the rest of the world may disagree, you still believe it to be a beautiful place.'*

Iain Thomas

Not long after starting my business, a lovely young woman in her early thirties, Reneé, came to see me, wanting to make a few small changes in her life. Beautiful inside and out, she had a wisdom beyond her years. As well as our coaching work together, she joined one of my first meditation groups and her presence in the room was a gift.

I got to know Reneé well in the months that followed. I listened as she described the gratitude she had for her life. She loved her work, her friends, live music and her family, and she said that the favourite part of her week was walking along the river with her mother on a Saturday morning. I hoped that when my own girls were her age we would share such a bond, and also that they would recognise, as Reneé did, that it's the small things that make life beautiful.

This thoughtful young woman had a kind word to say about everyone and I was touched by her generous and open heart.

Six months after our first meeting, I had a call from one of her colleagues to share the devastating news that Reneé had been involved in an accident and she hadn't survived. It seemed like a heartless injustice that the world had lost such a beautiful soul.

After her funeral service, I sent a note of condolence to her mother, Karen, who I later met. It was then that I learned how Reneé had come to be the person she was. Karen, who has since become my dearest friend, has the kindest heart of all time.

In her short life, Reneé embodied the philosophies of mindfulness, compassion and gratitude for the simple aspects of life. I took so much from knowing her.

Maybe the most significant lesson was the importance of finding beauty in everyday, ordinary things. We often work on our personal development goals thinking there'll be an endpoint where we have it all figured out and where life will be rosy and happy. After losing Reneé, I realised that genuine contentment is learning to be right here – to embrace this flawed and imperfect and very brief life and to find a way to love every part of it.

Something Reneé and I had in common was a desire to make every day beautiful, regardless of our external circumstances.

# Create a morning routine

Begin each day with a small amount of ritual. Meditate or practise gratitude for a few minutes upon waking. Eat breakfast mindfully. Walk, stretch or do some deep breathing before commencing your working day. Spend 30 minutes writing in your journal or planning your day. Create a simple, grounding routine and commit to it every morning.

# Take care of your body

## Move

One of the most effective ways to restore mental strength and boost your mood is to create more physical strength in your body. Choose an activity you genuinely enjoy rather than engaging in a form of movement just because it's what you think *you should be doing*. If you're not a typical athlete, try dancing, walking, yoga or qigong. Go gently if that feels preferable but remind yourself that a strong body helps to make a strong mind.

## Breathe deeply

Researchers have found that when we spend time on our devices, our posture changes and our breathing is much shallower (some people even hold their breath while emailing or texting). This puts additional stress on our immune system which in turn impacts our mood and our sleep and makes us more susceptible to anxiety and depression.

From time to time during your day, pause and check how you're breathing. Place one hand on your chest and one on your abdomen area. Breathe normally to see if you're using your diaphragm when breathing (if you are, the hand on your stomach will move and this means you're breathing fully).

Then spend a few minutes taking deep breaths into the abdomen area. Pause between the in- and out-breath and extend your out-breath so it's a little longer and slower than usual. Repeat this for five to seven breaths several times each day.

## Remember to physically relax

Most of us are unaware of how much physical tension we hold in our bodies and we miss the fact that this physical tension makes it difficult to mentally relax. Engage in a physical relaxation practice at least a few times each week. Listen to a body scan or yoga nidra meditation, take a bath, enjoy a massage or just lie on the grass in your local park and watch the clouds or the stars.

## Nourish your body

Eating is one of life's greatest pleasures, yet many of us forget to fully engage our senses to enjoy the simple experience of nourishing our bodies. Give your next meal your full attention and feel a sense of gratitude for all the people who have played a part in bringing food to your table. Put your devices away, slow down and savour everything you eat.

# Make your living environment beautiful

Even if your home is temporary, in need of renovating or imperfect in some way, do what you can to create a living environment that feels nurturing and welcoming. Light a scented candle or diffuse an essential oil to lift your mood. Buy yourself fresh flowers or an indoor plant. Tidy your wardrobe and declutter your living room. Turn on a lamp instead of your overhead lights. These small external changes will go a long way towards transforming your inner world.

## Spend time with people you genuinely love

Most of us don't need therapists to solve our problems but we do need people in our lives who listen and understand us well. Take stock of your relationships and make time for those that are genuinely supportive and reciprocal. If you feel lacking in terms of support, find a good therapist or coach and meet with them on a regular basis.

## Make peace with your life

There's a Buddhist notion that we're *already free*, regardless of our life circumstances. That everything we experience, all our joys and our suffering, contribute to the wholeness of life and that there's nothing we need to escape from.

We have a choice, every day, in how we interact with our lives. In the same way Viktor Frankl did, we find internal peace most readily when we accept that we're going to encounter adversity, grief and pain. It's only when we can soften into this knowing that we're able to embrace the concept of equanimity and find meaning in our experience of suffering.

Living this way might mean expending less energy wanting to *fix yourself* and less effort wanting to resolve your internal conflict. These are the very things that keep us from connecting with the people we love and noticing what's right in our lives. Instead, there is something of a surrendering to life, not because we are passive recipients, but rather because we recognise our sense of agency in choosing how we respond to things we know we can never change.

I know two women who have challenging relationships with their families. When Elizabeth visits her parents, she lets her mother's negativity get under her skin. She feels frustrated by her parents' constant bickering and she leaves feeling prickly and irritated. She goes home to complain to her husband and kids.

Sally, on the other hand, listens patiently while her mother unloads her most recent complaints. She doesn't take her parents arguing to heart and instead, occasionally teases them about it, breaking the ice with laughter. She keeps her visits short, gives both of her parents a loving hug, then makes the choice to leave their energy with them. As she walks back into her home, she feels an enormous sense of gratitude for the love she's created in her own little family.

'It is unconditional compassion for ourselves that leads naturally to unconditional compassion for others. If we are willing to stand fully in our own shoes and never give up on ourselves, then we will be able to put ourselves in the shoes of others and never give up on them.'

Pema Chödrön

When we are able to make room for the complexity of this experience we call 'life' and allow for the imperfection within all of us, maybe the best we can do is to offer ourselves and our loved ones *unconditional kindness.*

This soothes some of our inner turmoil and helps us to recognise when it's too much to manage on our own. Talking therapy is often helpful and maybe even medication, but there's also solace to be found in the ancient practices of meditation, yoga, spending time in nature and finding your own form of spirituality. They're the same practices that will guide you to a more conscious way of living, where you are less bound by societal expectations, more in tune with your own needs and more cognisant of what gives *your* life purpose and meaning.

Only then do we find we have the clarity to see what really matters. We don't need to be enraged by every injustice or engaged in every conflict, and we don't have to take every slight personally. With an open and loving heart, we're more able to see our own and others' goodness. We're more confident to set healthy boundaries and to make honest requests of the people we love. Instead of withdrawing in hurt or lashing out in anger, we're able to stay in the conversation and ask for the things that we want.

With this grounded and mindful approach, it's likely you'll find that you have the energy to live to your highest values, prioritise your valuable relationships and get solidly behind a few causes that really matter to you. And you'll do all of this imperfectly, but that's okay.

The wisest mindfulness teachers suggest that as well as living with kindness and equanimity, we should also remember not to take ourselves too seriously, to find lightness in our lives and make time to sing and dance and laugh and create.

I have an image in my mind of Reneé from a photo taken on a summer evening. She's on her way to a music concert, smiling widely across her shoulder. The look on her face is pure joy. She has the kind of energy you'd be happy to follow anywhere.

She used to say, 'Miracles happen every day . . . it's just that we don't see them.'

In many ways, the path to a meaningful life is uncomplicated. It's about recognising that the short amount of time we get to spend on this earth is a blessing. And we need to make as much of it as we can.

# References

Al Taher, Reham, 'The Classification of Character Strengths and Virtues', *Positive Psychology*, 1 September 2020, positivepsychology.com/classification-character-strengths-virtues, accessed 2020.

Biswas-Diener, Robert and Dean, Ben, *Positive Psychology Coaching: Putting the Science of Happiness to Work for Your Clients*, John Wiley & Sons, 2007.

Blakeslee, Sandra, 'In Work on Intuition, Gut Feelings Are Tracked to Source: The Brain', 4 March 1997, *New York Times*, www.nytimes.com/1997/03/04/science/in-work-on-intuition-gut-feelings-are-tracked-to-source-the-brain.html, accessed 2020.

Brach, Tara, *Radical Acceptance: Embracing Your Life with the Heart of a Buddha*, Bantam Books, 2003.

Brown, Joshua and Wong, Joel, 'How Gratitude Changes You and Your Brain', *Greater Good Magazine*, 6 June 2017, greatergood.berkeley.edu/article/item/how_gratitude_changes_you_and_your_brain, accessed 2020.

Bryant, Adam, 'Good C.E.O.'s Are Insecure (and Know It)', *New York Times*, 9 October 2010, www.nytimes.com/2010/10/10/business/10corner.html, accessed 2020.

Cacioppo, John, 'The lethality of loneliness' [Video file], TEDxDes Moines, 9 September 2013, www.youtube.com/watch?v=_0hxl03JoA0, accessed 2020.

Clear, James, *Atomic Habits: An Easy & Proven Way to Build Good Habits & Break Bad Ones*, Avery Publishing, 2018.

Colson, Thomas, 'This expert told us the secret to why Denmark is the happiest country in the world', *Business Insider Australia*, 15 September 2016, www.businessinsider. com.au/happiness-expert-meik-wiking-on-hygge-and-hugs-denmark-happiest-country-2016-9, accessed 2020.

Cook, Gareth, 'Why We Are Wired to Connect', *Scientific American*, 22 October 2013, www.scientificamerican.com/article/why-we-are-wired-to-connect, accessed 2020.

Crace, John, 'The Little Book of Lykke: The Danish Search for the World's Happiest People by Meik Wiking – digested read', *The Guardian*, 11 September 2017, www. theguardian.com/books/2017/sep/10/the-little-book-of-lykke-meik-wiking-danish-happiest-people-digested-read, accessed 2020.

Csikszentmihalyi, Mihaly, *Flow: The Psychology of Optimal Experience*, Harper Perennial, 1990.

Dweck, Carol, *Mindset: The New Psychology of Success*, Ballantine Books, 2006.

Edwards, Betty, *Drawing on the Right Side of the Brain*, Tarcher Books, 1979.

Fogg, B J, *Tiny Habits: The Small Changes That Change Everything*, Houghton Mifflin Harcourt, 2019.

Forsyth, John P and Eifert, Georg H, *The Mindfulness and Acceptance Workbook for Anxiety*, New Harbinger Publications, 2016.

Frankl, Viktor E, *Man's Search for Meaning*, Beacon Press, 1946.

Germer, Christopher, *The Mindful Path to Self-Compassion*, The Guildford Press, 2009.

Gladwell, Malcolm, *Blink: The Power of Thinking Without Thinking*, Back Bay Books, 2005.

Graham, Linda, 'How to Overcome Barriers to Forgiveness', *Greater Good Magazine*, 13 May 2014, greatergood.berkeley.edu/article/item/overcome_barriers_forgiveness, accessed 2020.

The Greater Good Science Center at the University of California, Berkeley, 'What is Forgiveness', *Greater Good Magazine*, greatergood.berkeley.edu/topic/forgiveness/definition#what-is-forgiveness, accessed 2020.

Hanson, Rick, *Buddha's Brain: the practical neuroscience of happiness, love & wisdom*, New Harbinger Publications, 2009.

Hanson, Rick, 'Forgive Yourself', *Psychology Today*, 22 July 2011, www.psychologytoday. com/au/blog/your-wise-brain/201107/forgive-yourself, accessed 2020.

Harris, Russ, *Act Made Simple: An Easy-to-Read Primer on Acceptance and Commitment Therapy*, New Harbinger Publications, 2009.

Harris, Russ, *The Happiness Trap: How to Stop Struggling and Start Living: A Guide to ACT*, Trumpeter Publishing, 2007.

Hoare, Judith, 'Face, accept, float, let time pass: Claire Weekes' anxiety cure holds true decades on', *Sydney Morning Herald*, 21 September 2019, www.smh.com.au/lifestyle/

health-and-wellness/face-accept-float-let-time-pass-claire-weekes-anxiety-cure-holds-true-decades-on-20190917-p52s2w.html, accessed 2020.

'Internal Family Systems (IFS)', *Good Therapy*, www.goodtherapy.org/learn-about-therapy/types/internal-family-systems-therapy, accessed 2020.

Jarrett, Christian, 'The Transformational Power of How You Talk About Your Life', *BBC Future*, 27 May 2019, www.bbc.com/future/story/20190523-the-way-you-tell-your-life-story-shapes-your-personality, accessed 2020.

Kabat-Zinn, Jon, *Full Catastrophe Living: Using the Wisdom of Your Body and Mind to Face Stress, Pain, and Illness*, Delta Press, 1990.

Khazan, Olga, 'How Loneliness Begets Loneliness', *The Atlantic*, 6 April 2017, www.theatlantic.com/health/archive/2017/04/how-loneliness-begets-loneliness/521841, accessed 2020.

Kornfield, Jack, *A Path with Heart*, Bantam Books, 1993.

University of Leeds, 'Go with your gut – intuition is more than just a hunch, says Leeds research', 5 March 2008, www.leeds.ac.uk/news/article/367/go_with_your_gut__intuition_is_more_than_just_a_hunch_says_leeds_research, accessed 2020.

Lieberman, Matthew, *Social – Why Our Brains Are Wired to Connect*, Crown Publishing, 2013.

Locke, E A, Shaw, K N, Saari, L M, and Latham, G P, 'Goal setting and task performance: 1969–1980', *Psychological Bulletin*, 90(1), 125–152, doi.org/10.1037/0033-2909.90.1.125, accessed 2020.

Malkin, Craig, 'Five Ways to Overcome Feelings of Neediness', *Psychology Today*, 30 November 2012, www.psychologytoday.com/us/blog/romance-redux/201211/five-ways-overcome-feelings-neediness, accessed 2020.

McLeod, Saul, 'Cognitive Behavioral Therapy', *Simply Psychology*, updated 2019, www.simplypsychology.org/cognitive-therapy.html, accessed 2020

Melemis, Steven, *I Want to Change My Life: How to Overcome Anxiety, Depression and Addiction*, Modern Therapies, 2010.

Muth, Jon J, *Zen Shorts*, Scholastic Press, 2005.

Neff, Kristin, 'What self-compassion is', *Self-Compassion*, self-compassion.org/the-three-elements-of-self-compassion-2, accessed 2020.

Pennock, Seph Fontane, 'The Hedonic Treadmill – Are We Forever Chasing Rainbows?', *Positive Psychology*, 1 September 2020, positivepsychology.com/hedonic-treadmill, accessed 2020.

Randolph, Keith, 'Sports Visualizations', *Llywellyn Encyclopedia*, 15 May 2002, www.llewellyn.com/encyclopedia/article/244, accessed 2020.

Richardson, Cheryl, *Stand Up for Your Life: A Practical Step-by-Step Plan to Build Inner Confidence and Personal Power*, Free Press, 2002.

Ross, Will, 'What is Irrational?', *REBT Network*, 2006, www.rebtnetwork.org/library/ideas.html, accessed 2020.

Ruch, Willibald and Proyer, René T, 'Mapping strengths into virtues: the relation of the 24 VIA-strengths to six ubiquitous virtues', *Frontiers in Psychology*, 6:640, 21 April 2015, doi.org/10.3389/fpsyg.2015.00460, accessed 2020.

Sakulku, Jaruwan and Alexander, James, 'The Impostor Phenomenon', *International Journal of Behavioural Science*, 2011, vol. 6, no. 1, 75–97, so06.tci-thaijo.org/index. php/IJBS/article/view/521/pdf, accessed 2020.

Schwartz, Richard, *Greater Than the Sum of Our Part: Discovering Your True Self through Internal Family Systems Therapy*, Sounds True, 2018.

Schwartz, Richard, 'The Internal Family Systems Model Outline', *Internal Family Systems Institute*, ifs-institute.com/resources/articles/internal-family-systems-model-outline, accessed 2020.

'Science Explains Why Grateful People Live Longer', *Power of Positivity*, www.power ofpositivity.com/grateful-people-why-live-longer, accessed 2020.

Seligman, Martin E P, *Authentic Happiness: Using the New Positive Psychology to Realize Your Potential for Lasting Fulfillment*, Atria Books, 2002.

Seligman, Martin E P, *Flourish*, Free Press, 2011.

Seligman, Martin E P, *Learned Optimism: How to Change Your Mind and Your Life*, Vintage, 1990.

Stone, Hal and Sidra, *Embracing Your Inner Critic: Turning Self-Criticism into a Creative Asset*, Harper One, 1993.

Texas A&M University, 'We are all 'wired' for addiction, says researcher', *Science Daily*, 24 August 2016, www.sciencedaily.com/releases/2016/08/160824172706.htm, accessed 2020.

Treder-Wolff, Jude, 'The Therapeutic Benefits Of Telling Your Stories', *Medium*, 8 January 2017, medium.com/@judetrederwolff/the-therapeutic-benefits-of-telling-your-stories-3244a07af60d, accessed 2020.

van Cuylenburg, Hugh, *The Resilience Project: Finding Happiness through Gratitude, Empathy and Mindfulness*, Ebury Australia, 2019.

Wiking, Miek, *The Little Book of Lykke: The Danish Search for the World's Happiest People*, Penguin Life, 2017.

Wiseman, Richard, *The Luck Factor: Changing Your Luck, Changing Your Life – The Four Essential Principles*, Miramax, 2003.

Young, Valerie, 'The 5 Types of Impostors', impostorsyndrome.com/5-types-of-impostors, accessed 2020.

Young, Valerie, *The Secret Thoughts of Successful Women: Why Capable People Suffer from the Impostor Syndrome and How to Thrive in Spite of It*, Crown Business, 2011.

Zander, Benjamin and Rosamund, *The Art of Possibility: Transforming Personal and Professional Life*, Penguin, 2000.

# Text Acknowledgements

Meg's story on pages 224-225 kindly shared with permission.
'Face Your Fear' game on page 231-34 from *Stand Up for Your Life*. Copyright © 2002
   by Cheryl Richardson. Reprinted by permission of the author.
'Forgive Yourself' exercise on pages 245-47 from https://www.rickhanson.net/forgive-
   yourself-now/. Copyright © Rick Hanson. Reprinted by permission of the author.
Reneé's story on pages 255-256 kindly shared with permission.

# Acknowledgements

Writing this book and working with the wonderful team at Pan Macmillan has been an absolute joy. Huge thanks to Ingrid Ohlsson for giving me the nudge I needed to write this book. I'm especially grateful that you encouraged me to share my work in this way and write in my own voice.

Thank you to Naomi van Groll for your creative direction, your kindness and for working so closely with me to make every aspect of the book the best it could possibly be.

Thank you to Brianne Collins for your wonderful edit and to Rebecca Lay for your help with permissions. Thanks also to Candice Wyman and Adrik Kemp for getting the book out into the world and to Belinda Huang and Milly Ivanovic for keeping things humming away in the background.

Huge thanks to the lovely Kelly Exeter for so generously supporting me with writing and research while you were in the midst of a great challenge of your own.

A big thank you to Lydia Batts for the beautiful watercolour painting on the cover and to Emily O'Neill for your lovely design work.

Special thanks to my dear friend Catherine Morey-Nase for reviewing the inner critic chapter and for the hours spent chatting about all of the concepts I've included in the book. You are such a kindred spirit and your friendship is the greatest gift.

Thank you to Carrie Hayward for checking the ACT and CBT chapters for accuracy and for being such a generous and kind colleague and friend.

To Robert Rabbin, who is no longer with us, thank you for making me believe I had something to say and for teaching me to be brave enough to stand on a stage in front of hundreds of people without fear. I miss you greatly every day.

Thank you to Barb Long for your wisdom on our weekly walks. What a blessing to have had you in my 25 km zone during lockdown.

Thanks to Trish Weston for being my go-to person for anything to do with books and personal development. I wish you every success with Bibliocoach where you combine both.

Thank you to my parents for your open-minded thinking and for encouraging independence. I'm so grateful to have had the freedom to choose my own path.

And the biggest thanks to my own little family who are always so patient when my time is taken up with writing. To Chris, for the endless cups of teapot tea, for cooking on the nights I worked late and for taking care of the chickens and the garden while I've had less time to get outside. How lucky I am to have you.

To our gorgeous girls Elsa and Meg, for listening to my ideas, for your belief in me, for making me laugh and for your abundance of love and support.

And huge thanks to Toby and our precious grandchildren Oscar and Milla, for being a constant source of joy.

And finally, deep gratitude to my dearest friend Karen Ramaekers, who was kind enough to let me share the story of her beautiful girl Reneé in the final chapter. Meeting you both changed my life.